Partners in Teaching and Learning

Beta Phi Mu Scholars series

Founded in 1948, Beta Phi Mu is the international library and information studies honor society. Its mission is to recognize and encourage scholastic achievement among library and information studies students.

The Beta Phi Mu Scholars series publishes significant contributions and substantive advances in the field of library and information science. Series editor Andrea Falcone is committed to presenting work which reflects Beta Phi Mu's commitments to scholarship, leadership, and service. The series fosters creative, innovative, and well-articulated works that members of the field will find influential.

Recently published titles in the series are:

Book Banning in 21st-Century America by Emily J. M. Knox
Young Adult Literature, Libraries, and Conservative Activism by Loretta M. Gaffney
School Librarianship: Past, Present, and Future Edited by Susan W. Alman
Six Issues Facing Libraries Today: Critical Perspectives by John Budd
Access to Information, Technology, and Justice: A Critical Intersection by Ursula Gorham
Academic Library Metamorphosis and Regeneration by Marcy Simons
Collaborations for Student Success: How Librarians and Student Affairs Work Together to Enrich Learning by Dallas Long
Partners in Teaching and Learning: Coordinating a Successful Academic Library Instruction Program by Melissa Mallon

Partners in Teaching and Learning

Coordinating a Successful Academic Library Instruction Program

Melissa N. Mallon

ROWMAN & LITTLEFIELD
Lanham • Boulder • New York • London

Published by Rowman & Littlefield
An imprint of The Rowman & Littlefield Publishing Group, Inc.
4501 Forbes Boulevard, Suite 200, Lanham, Maryland 20706
www.rowman.com

6 Tinworth Street, London SE11 5AL, United Kingdom

Copyright © 2020 by The Rowman & Littlefield Publishing Group, Inc.

All rights reserved. No part of this book may be reproduced in any form or by any electronic or mechanical means, including information storage and retrieval systems, without written permission from the publisher, except by a reviewer who may quote passages in a review.

British Library Cataloguing in Publication Information Available

Library of Congress Cataloging-in-Publication Data

Names: Mallon, Melissa N., author
Title: Partners in teaching and learning : coordinating a successful academic library instruction program / Melissa Mallon.
Description: Lanham : Rowman & Littlefield, [2020] | Series: Beta Phi Mu scholars series | Includes bibliographical references and index. | Summary: "Instruction coordinators and directors in academic libraries may have a variety of titles and wear an entire wardrobe's worth of hats, but we face many of the same challenges in developing, promoting, and evaluating our instruction programs."—Provided by publisher.
Identifiers: LCCN 2020006324 (print) | LCCN 2020006325 (ebook) | ISBN 9781538118832 (cloth) | ISBN 9781538118849 (paperback) | ISBN 9781538118856 (epub)
Subjects: LCSH: Academic libraries—Relations with faculty and curriculum—United States. | Information literacy—Study and teaching (Higher)—United States. | Information literacy—Study and teaching (Higher)—United States—Evaluation | Instruction librarians—Professional relationships—United States.
Classification: LCC Z675.U5 M3268 2020 (print) | LCC Z675.U5 (ebook) | DDC 027.7—dc23
LC record available at https://lccn.loc.gov/2020006324
LC ebook record available at https://lccn.loc.gov/2020006325

Contents

List of Figures, Tables, and Textboxes		vii
Preface		ix
Acknowledgments		xi
Introduction		xiii
1	The Intentional Instruction Coordinator	1
2	Taking Stock of an Instruction Program	17
3	Creating a Culture of Teaching and Learning in the Library	29
4	To Frame or Not to Frame?	41
5	Writing an Instruction Program Statement	51
6	Advocating for an Instruction Program	61
7	Assessing an Instruction Program	73
8	When an Instruction Program Goes Astray	89
9	Growing as an Instruction Coordinator	105
Conclusion		117
Appendix: An Instruction Coordinator's Bookshelf		123
References		125
Index		137
About the Author		141

List of Figures, Tables, and Textboxes

FIGURE

Figure 6.1　Instruction Program Advocacy Map　　　　　　64

TABLES

Table 7.1　Sample Instruction Program Learning Outcomes　　82–83
Table 8.1　Asking Difficult Questions About an Instruction Program　　93–95

TEXTBOXES

Textbox 1.1　Put It in Practice: Are You an Intentional Instruction Coordinator?　　12
Textbox 2.1　Put It in Practice: The 5Ws Campus Scan　　23
Textbox 8.1　Psychological Safety and Difficult Conversations　　96
Textbox 9.1　Put It in Practice: Identifying Burnout　　107
Textbox 9.2　Selected Library Instruction Conferences　　113
Textbox 9.3　Selected Higher Education and Leadership Conferences　　114

Preface

Throughout my career, I have worked in academic institutions of varying shapes and sizes, from private universities to small branch libraries. I have also held a variety of library roles related to teaching and research support, including working as a subject librarian, coordinating small and large instruction programs, and directing a multilibrary system teaching and learning program. When I started my first Instruction Coordinator position, I didn't have a template or a roadmap that told me exactly how to do my job. And it wasn't easy: I encountered faculty that had certain expectations for their classes, and coworkers who were passionate about their work but also suffering from burn out. My colleagues from library school were full of excitement and stories about their library instruction adventures, which left me wondering if I was doing something wrong. I was still learning how to be a teacher in my own right, while simultaneously determining how to integrate information literacy into the curriculum, assess student learning, and teach my colleagues about information literacy pedagogy. I quickly realized that while my situation was wildly different than many of my counterparts in other libraries, it was also a fairly common scenario in many academic libraries. Over time, I have also come to realize that while I didn't have a handy roadmap when I was starting in my first coordinator position, the freedom to learn and grow on my own also pushed me to expand my understanding and preconceived notions of "library instruction" and what it meant to lead a library instruction program.

This book is designed to explore and unpack what it means to lead a successful library instruction program for new Instruction Coordinators, but also for librarians that have been coordinating or directing instruction programs for some time. Grounded in literature from library science, organizational and leadership development, higher education research and practice, and the scholarship of teaching and learning, as well as weaving in my own professional experience, this book provides strategies for nurturing the pedagogical skills of librarians and discusses how to contextualize an instruction program within both the library and the larger institution, all while advocating for the criticality of librarians as partners in teaching and learning.

One caveat, however, on what this book is *not*; it is not meant to be a how-to manual, and thus readers will not find a book full of templates and guidelines that are prescriptive as to how one should lead an instruction program. This book is also not meant to dictate any one "best" way to lead a teaching and learning program or what that program "should" look like, because, let's be honest, there is no one best way. Rather, an Instruction Coordinator must determine the context of their teaching and learning environment from the micro and macro levels and adjust their programmatic strategy to fit this environment. Coordinators may find themselves engaging in this work with an entire team of librarians or they may be working alone. Regardless, this book outlines several flexible strategies and approaches that can help an Instruction Coordinator, either new or veteran, determine the contextually appropriate methods for infusing information literacy instruction into the fabric of the library and the campus within which it sits.

Regardless of their role or title within their organizational hierarchy, Instruction Coordinators are, without a doubt, leaders in their libraries. Moreover, they are well poised to position the libraries, and thus the library's teaching efforts, as an important and crucial contributor to student learning within the higher education landscape. This book furthers this conversation by emphasizing the importance of building partnerships, of meeting colleagues where they are, and of creating an inclusive and welcoming culture for not only teaching librarians but also students, faculty, staff, and administrators.

Acknowledgments

Many, many thanks go out to the editors of the Beta Phi Mu Scholars Series, Andrea Falcone and Jennifer Leffler, for their unwavering enthusiasm and guidance, and for asking critical and thought-provoking questions. Thank you also, to Beta Phi Mu, for sponsoring the contest that started this journey.

Thank you to my fellow alumna of the Harvard Leadership Institute for Academic Librarians, Melanie Maksin, for helping make this book a reality, and for our many thought-provoking conversations about the library's integral role in teaching and learning.

I would also like to thank Karen Swoopes at Vanderbilt's Peabody Library, Dr. Julie Roberts, and Megan Mallon for their support and encouragement during the writing of this book. And, as always, thank you to my partner, William Caldwell, for always being there and helping me achieve balance.

Introduction

The goal of this book is to provide a roadmap for the successful development and maintenance of a library's teaching and learning program. There are many books and articles that focus on information literacy programs for specific disciplines and on the importance of information literacy instruction in higher education; this book examines an academic library's teaching and learning program from a wider, institutional lens. Rather than focusing solely on information literacy, this text explores the academic library's more comprehensive role in teaching and learning on campus. Readers will find techniques and resources for advancing a library's teaching and learning agenda, including planning an instruction program, creating a mission and vision statement for the program, marketing and advocating for the program, and creating an inclusive community of teachers within the library. The chapters contain practical resources and tools for librarians leading instruction programs; for example, activities for engaging librarians in program development, strategies for advocacy, creating an inclusive community of teachers, and frameworks for program assessment. These sections are bookended by a discussion of the importance of the Instruction Coordinator's role in overseeing an instruction program and how to be successful in this role.

The Preface introduced several questions that help set the stage for the who and/or what an Instruction Coordinator is; Chapter 1 also explores this question. Crucially, this book does not intend to advocate or push a particular definition or expectation of an Instruction Coordinator, because there are many ways to approach this work. The role may be specifically defined (as in, a job title of *Instruction Coordinator*), or a library may not have an explicit Coordinator, but rather someone who leads informally, or guides teaching efforts as part of a larger portfolio. An individual librarian tasked with leading and teaching the entirety of an instruction program should also feel encouraged to use this book in ways that will benefit themselves and their program.

Additionally, it is worth stressing that while this book does not provide a hard and fast definition of who or what an Instruction Coordinator is, it does examine what it means to coordinate or lead an instruction program, and what it means to be successful in that task. To help facilitate this discussion, it is worth spending a few moments discussing what differentiates an instruction program (singular) from instruction programs (plural).

When writing about an *instruction program*, the author takes a holistic view of teaching and learning within an academic library. There may be numerous components of the program, including coordination of and participation in multiple instructional efforts, but the components can be seen to relate to the whole. *Instruction programs*, on the other hand, may consist of a piecemeal assortment of instructional offerings. These individual sessions or programs may be thoughtfully designed and make contributions to student learning; however, they are disconnected from one another and lack a cohesive vision of the role of the library in campus teaching and learning endeavors.

The key here is that the definition of an *instruction program* may be very different depending on institutional context. Documents such as the Association of College and Research Libraries' (ACRL) *Guidelines for Instruction Programs in Academic Libraries* (2011) and the *Characteristics of Programs of Information Literacy That Illustrate Best Practices: A Guideline* (2019) provide guidance on the characteristics of what constitutes a successful instruction program, but there are still no established or universally accepted definitions for what a program actually *is*. This is because an instruction program is entirely contextual for each institution. Possible formats of programs and their leadership could be:

- **formal:** an established instruction program with a Coordinator or director and librarians whose roles are explicitly dedicated to teaching information literacy;
- **informal:** no articulated Coordinator role; the library's teaching efforts may be led by an associate dean or public services department head;
- **small:** made up of a single person or a few librarians who share the teaching load (these roles could be formal or informal); and
- **large:** perhaps comprised of a liaison program, with librarians assigned to each department, or an instruction program that has dedicated teams for undergraduate students/graduate students, etc.

Or any number of other organizational combinations. In this book, the author explores the concept of an instruction program as a whole; rather than zeroing in on how an instruction program *should* be organized, as well as the components that Coordinators should consider to lead a successful instruction program—no matter what that program looks like.

HOW TO READ THIS BOOK

Before introducing the different chapters, it may be helpful to examine how this book is organized and, in turn, how readers might approach the joyful task of engaging with this book. As discussed, in addition to the variety and formality of Instruction Coordinator roles, there are also many types of instruction programs in academic libraries. Woven throughout this book are discussions about certain aspects of program management, but readers are encouraged to think creatively about how the strategies and techniques can apply to their own institutional contexts. Several ways are provided to help readers think about certain challenges and opportunities in leading an instruction program, but there is no way to create alternatives for every known (and unknown) type of instruction program organization. That being said, readers should find enough generalized information to be able to apply the content to their own institutional context.

Additionally, as a reminder from the Preface, this book is not meant to be read as a "how-to" manual; rather, the reader will find prompts and questions to spark curiosity and an invitation to delve deeper into what it means to be an active and intentional leader of teaching and learning both within an academic library and on campus.

CHAPTER OVERVIEWS

Just like teaching is ever-evolving, coordinating an instruction program requires much in the way of ideation, experimentation, and evaluation. With that in mind, many components of this book's overall theme (coordinating a successful academic library instruction program) are discussed in multiple contexts. Each chapter dives a little deeper into a specific aspect related to directing or coordinating library teaching and learning programs that will ultimately impact its success.

The Intentional Instruction Coordinator

Chapter 1 follows up on the questions and assumptions about the Instruction Coordinator that have been introduced thus far. It will be especially useful for anyone stepping into, or wanting to step into, a leadership role in a teaching and learning program, whether that happens through the development of a new instruction program or a move into a new position. This chapter details the transition from instructor to Coordinator/director/leader and provides strategies for flexing teaching muscles, pedagogical know-how, and leadership skills to develop a program and support an instruction team. Finally, it discusses the mindset and dispositions of intentional Instruction Coordinators.

Taking Stock of an Instruction Program

This chapter introduces the concept of the environmental scan; this is an important foundational process for Instruction Coordinators and those leading instruction programs. Chapter 2 will help readers chart the landscape of teaching and learning in their library and on campus, while encouraging reflection on the people and resources needed to coordinate or direct a successful instruction program. The author recommends approaching this process as inclusively as possible, by involving the many constituents that have a stake in the program's success.

Creating a Culture of Teaching and Learning in the Library

Despite the wide variety of instruction program types (e.g., small, large, liaison structure, distributed), the culture in which that program is situated will greatly impact its direction and success. This chapter covers many approaches for fostering and sustaining a culture of teaching and learning in the library, including the importance of professional development for teaching librarians and the creation of Communities of Practice focusing on teaching and pedagogy. This chapter also examines how incorporating teaching styles and preferences of a variety of instruction librarians (including subject liaisons, scholarly communications, digital scholarship, etc.) will strengthen and extend the reach of the instruction program.

To Frame or Not to Frame?

The ACRL *Framework for Information Literacy for Higher Education* (ACRL *Framework*) (and before it, the ACRL *Information Literacy Competency Standards for Higher Education* [ACRL *Standards*]) is widely seen as a guiding document for library instruction, both for individual sessions and for instruction programs. This chapter provides an analytical approach to using the ACRL *Framework* as a foundational document on which to build an instruction program. On the one hand, it can provide a shared understanding on which to base student learning outcomes and instruction program statements. Conversely, if those same learning outcomes and statements do not mention the ACRL *Framework* (or even the term "information literacy"), is it still an instruction program? (The author's answer? Yes!) Chapter 4 discusses the importance of understanding an institution's teaching culture, along with strategies for gaining that crucial understanding, to build the foundation for the instruction program.

Writing an Instruction Program Statement

On the heels of the conversation about incorporating the ACRL *Framework* or similar guiding documents or approaches, Chapter 5 tackles the issue of the instruction program statement. This chapter covers suggested elements of an instruction program statement, as well as discusses how a strong statement can also help guide Instruction Coordinators in articulating a vision for teaching and learning. The author makes recommendations for fostering an inclusive process for drafting the program statement and suggests how teaching librarians and other partners play a role in turning the instruction program statement and vision into reality.

Advocating for an Instruction Program

Articulating the instruction program's statement and mission or vision is crucial, but how does the Instruction Coordinator then use that statement in their communication and marketing for the program? Advocating for the library's role in teaching and learning is an important component for those that lead instruction programs; Chapter 6 discusses this advocacy role, as well as some of the differences between advocacy, marketing, and promotion. It also provides strategies for developing consistent, relevant messages about an instruction program, and articulating the importance of engaging stakeholders to advocate for and promote the library's impact on teaching and learning.

Assessing an Instruction Program

Teaching librarians are no strangers to assessment; they have devised many ways to creatively and authentically assess student learning, both in individual sessions and across the curriculum. This chapter takes those principles and applies them to program assessment. How does an Instruction Coordinator develop and assess program learning outcomes? How do "assessment" and "evaluation" differ, and how might an Instruction Coordinator define and measure the success of a program? How does the assessment done by individual teaching librarians impact the assessment of the instruction program as a whole? Chapter 7 answers these questions using a variety of techniques such as benchmarking and backward design.

When an Instruction Program Goes Astray

Just like in lesson planning and course design, Instruction Coordinators need to continuously monitor the forward momentum of their instruction program. No one likes to think about things going badly, but it can happen. Chapter 8 explores what happens if/when the library's course-integrated information literacy sessions, workshops, or other instructional efforts aren't as successful as they once were. This chapter also presents strategies for diagnosing common issues in instruction programs and offers suggestions for addressing individual and interpersonal challenges among instruction librarians. Additionally, various methods are shared for righting the ship when things go astray while remaining mindful of programmatic goals.

Growing as an Instruction Coordinator

Just as the first chapter touches on the Instruction Coordinator as an individual, the final chapter circles back to this role. Chapter 9 discusses techniques for personal development as a leader/director/coordinator, including strategies for recovering from burnout and opportunities for conferences, publications, and professional networks to sustain one's excitement and ongoing development. An intentional, engaged Instruction Coordinator is one who prioritizes personal and professional development, renews their focus, and strengthens relationships—resulting in a positive impact on their instruction program.

PARTNERS IN TEACHING AND LEARNING

The word *partners* was explicitly chosen for the title of this book because leading an academic library instruction program is not a solo responsibility. Regardless of organizational structure or program type, a library's teaching efforts are only as successful as the partnerships and collaborations that support and sustain a lasting impact on student learning. As the ACRL *Guidelines for Instruction Programs* (2011) (ACRL *Guidelines*) state:

> academic libraries work together with other members of their institutional communities to participate in, support, and achieve the educational mission of their institutions by teaching the core competencies of information literacy—the abilities involved in identifying an information need, accessing needed information, evaluating, managing, and applying information, and understanding the legal, social, and ethical aspects of information use. (para. 1)

While the definition of what makes an "information literate" person may morph and grow, the importance of working together will remain, and Instruction Coordinators are in a perfect position to foster these partnerships.

The strategies and techniques discussed in this book are meant to explore these collaborations, while also providing a roadmap for librarians that are leading, directing, or coordinating an academic library instruction program in articulating the importance of the library's role in teaching and learning.

Chapter One

The Intentional Instruction Coordinator

WHAT IS AN INSTRUCTION COORDINATOR?

In academic libraries, there are many names for, and varieties of, what is, in this book, referred to as an "Instruction Coordinator." There are coordinators, leaders, heads, assistant directors, directors, and more. The work under their purview may fall under information literacy, instruction, reference and instruction, teaching and learning, user education, research (or the broader "public") services, some combination of these, or something else entirely. Some Instruction Coordinators oversee a program with a professional staff of two, or four, or thirty. Some directly supervise librarians; some do not. Some are fully immersed in instruction, while others coordinate their organization's instruction program as part of a broader portfolio.

The complexity of the Instruction Coordinator role exists within innumerable variations on the idea of the library's instruction program. The library's instruction program may consist of library- or research-specific learning outcomes embedded in the curriculum, targeted information literacy instruction, which is scaffolded throughout a major or degree program, partnerships with individual faculty related to specific courses, credit-bearing courses on research methods, or something more complex and/or nuanced. Given the incredible diversity of teaching and learning efforts in academic libraries, it is unsurprising that, as Benjes-Small and Miller (2017) note, "there is no standard structure for how instruction-related activities and responsibilities are managed within a library" (p. 144).

While the program structures and their overseers' titles vary, there are a few hallmarks of the Coordinator role as it relates to leading an instruction program. The Association of College and Research Libraries' (ACRL) *Roles and Strengths of Teaching Librarians*[1] (ACRL *Roles and Strengths*) describes the role of teaching librarian as Coordinator:

> A coordinator leads, develops, and maintains a library and/or institution's information literacy program. This role requires highly effective organizational and communication skills in managing multiple simultaneous projects, events, resources, assessment, statistical reporting, and coordinating with administrators as well as academic departments. The coordinator must have diplomatic people skills and confidently navigate the politics of instruction, understanding the climate, culture, and expectations of the stakeholders involved in the institution's information literacy goals. (Amsberry et al., 2017, p. 6)

Benjes-Small and Miller (2017) emphasize four areas of many Instruction Coordinators' portfolios: "assessing and evaluating impact, collaborating, being strategic and programmatic, and leadership and mentorship" (p. 145). Hinchliffe (2016a) adds nuance to these more generic descriptions in a blog post about her own position, in which she highlights her focus on building "reliable and robust instructional infrastructures" for her institution's teaching librarians, as well as her role in "bring[ing] the lens of teaching and learning" to other projects and initiatives undertaken by her library, not just those related to instruction (para. 7, para. 10; cited in Benjes-Small & Miller, 2017, p. 143). Generally speaking, the Instruction Coordinator role in an academic library entails responsibility for programmatic aspects of instruction and includes providing a voice for teaching and learning within the library as well as amplifying the library in an institution's wider landscape of teaching and learning.

TRANSITIONING FROM INSTRUCTOR TO COORDINATOR

Many of those who coordinate academic library instruction programs were once solely instruction librarians themselves, and are fortunate in that their roles align with the element of academic librarianship that most excites, challenges, and satisfies them: teaching and learning. However, the move from teacher to Coordinator (or, in some cases, the addition of the responsibility for coordinating a program) is often a significant transition for librarians to navigate. It is far more than just a title change; it carries new responsibilities, some of which may be entirely unfamiliar or unanticipated, as well as the need for new behaviors and dispositions. For many Instruction Coordinators, this role may be the first in which they supervise other professionals and participate in their organization's middle management or leadership structure. It may also be the first time in which they lead ongoing, larger-scale initiatives, as opposed to smaller projects or programs. In many libraries, coordinating an instruction program does not always equal direct supervision of staff, but does require building consensus and garnering buy-in from peers who contribute to the instruction program. The position often requires working closely with administrators inside and outside the library, as opposed to focusing communication efforts on individual faculty members or departments, which can be difficult to scale up. Another change is that Instruction Coordinator positions rely less on subject knowledge and teaching ability than on skills related to diplomacy, advocacy, and coaching. Finally, for many librarians, taking on a coordinator or director role may signify the first time they are managing spaces, technology resources, and perhaps even a budget.

Stepping fully into the Instruction Coordinator role entails developing and implementing a vision, building and supporting a program, and bringing the library into the teaching and learning life of the institution. This transition from teacher to Coordinator, with its ambitious agenda and new demands, almost always involves letting go. Whether it is letting go of individual teaching responsibilities, letting go of one-on-one relationships with students and faculty, letting go of one's identity as a teacher first and foremost, or some combination of the above, the transition can be painful. Brown (2018) explains the importance of the transition from individual contributor to leader in a workplace:

> In a daring leadership role, it's time to lift up our teams and help them shine. This is one of the most difficult hurdles of advancement, particularly for those of us who are used to hustling, or don't know exactly where we contribute value once the areas where we contributed value before are delegated to those coming up behind us. (Brown, 2018, p. 109)

For the Instruction Coordinator who was once a "hustling" teaching librarian, it may be easier to let go if they have been hired at a new-to-them institution. When they interviewed for the position, they likely responded to questions about how they planned to make the transition from instruction librarian to Coordinator; at the very least, they would have likely given this some thought as part of their move to a new organization. The new Coordinator may have weighed the pros and cons and considered what they would be giving up (and gaining) to assume this role.

For the Instruction Coordinator who is promoted from within, those calculations may be less considered and more ad hoc. Some Instruction Coordinators may be expected to continue with their instructional responsibilities, but others may find themselves teaching "just this one class," even when it is more appropriate to assign the session to another member of the instruction team. That one class is a teaching opportunity for an instruction librarian; for the Coordinator, it is an opportunity to practice being the "guide on the side" instead of the "sage on the stage" within the instruction team. An internally promoted Instruction Coordinator may need to focus, particularly in their early months in the role, on trusting and developing their team, and on maintaining a bigger picture focus on the instruction program.

If letting go is part of the transition from instructor to Coordinator, so too is the process of discerning which skills, practices, and values to take into the new role. The Instruction Coordinator who has grown and developed as a library instructor is not starting over at the very beginning. A great teacher can take their strengths out of the classroom and into a variety of other contexts, including the realms of instruction program advocacy and professional development for others who teach. Connections between teaching and instruction program leadership are explored below (see "Teaching as Leadership") and in chapters 3, 4, and 6.

While the transition from instructor to one coordinating an instruction program can be professionally and personally challenging, the rewards of this transition can be immense. The Instruction Coordinator is in a position to shape the teaching and learning culture of their library and to advocate for the library's role in students' academic and personal growth. They have an opportunity to train and mentor instruction librarians and to share their own knowledge and passion on a wider scale. The Coordinator is uniquely equipped to engage with instruction in a potentially transformative way.

TRANSITIONING TO THE WORLD OF TEACHING AND LEARNING

What about the Instruction Coordinator for whom the instruction program is just one aspect of a larger portfolio? For this Coordinator, the transition might not involve letting go of a valued part of this daily work, but instead adding onto an already full plate of responsibilities. Perhaps their passion lies not with instruction, but with collection development (or access services, or digital scholarship, or another aspect of contemporary librarianship). In this case, the transition will involve the Coordinator making use of their best management and leadership strategies, but should also include a deep, thoughtful foray into teaching and learning within the contexts of academic librarianship and higher education. This book provides grounding in issues and approaches related to academic library instruction programs; it is recommended that readers drill down into several key works related to pedagogy within and beyond the library context, as well (see Appendix, "An Instruction Coordinator's Bookshelf"). Although one does not need to be, or to become, an instruction librarian to lead a successful library instruction program, familiarity with the state of the profession of academic librarianship and contemporary practices, as well as an appreciation for the work of their team of librarians, can only enrich the Coordinator's strategic thinking, mentoring, and advocacy related to teaching and learning in their library.

Even Instruction Coordinators with a thorough background in library instruction can benefit from looking beyond the library context and into higher education writ large (see Appendix). Keeping abreast of changing student demographics, emerging trends in assessment, current discussions related to pedagogy and the science of learning, and nurturing one's own network among teaching faculty and instructional support offices will provide valuable insight into the needs, pressures, and opportunities faced by colleges and universities as they enact their educational missions. This deeper understanding can help the Instruction Coordinator more effectively position their library as a partner in teaching and learning on campus.

LEADERSHIP MODELS FOR INSTRUCTION COORDINATORS

The management and leadership responsibilities of the Instruction Coordinator will vary across institutions and instruction programs, but these are often the most profound differences between the librarian role and the Coordinator role. The Instruction Coordinator is often, but not always, both a manager and a leader, balancing the day-to-day running of a program with "the dreams, visions, and desires to make a difference" (Grassian & Kaplowitz, 2005, p. 2). Regardless of their place in the organizational hierarchy, the Instruction Coordinator who takes on the mantle of leadership might consider a variety of models, or incorporate aspects of several models into their leadership practice. The two examples of leadership models that follow are especially resonant for academic library instruction programs.

Teaching as Leadership

As leaders, Instruction Coordinators might draw on their own teaching skills, as well as the central premise of "instructional leadership," to advance their library's teaching and learning mission.

Good teaching and good leadership are not dissimilar, according to Bahls (2016), and maintaining a connection to teaching can enhance one's leadership acumen. Bahls (2016), a college president, returned to the classroom and let go of the Socratic method, which he had previously favored in his classes and in his interactions with faculty and fellow administrators. He was inspired by another faculty member who employed facilitative and listening skills to generate "deep engagement and thought-provoking conversations" while remaining attuned to the students' "level of learning" (Bahls, 2016). Bahls saw that these same methods would be beneficial when discussing complex financial and organizational issues with faculty. Similarly, an Instruction Coordinator might think of conversations with their team as a context for teaching and learning, with the Coordinator as both the teacher, engaging others in rich conversations, and as the learner, listening and synthesizing for deeper understanding.

In his work on learning organizations, Senge (1990) proposes that one role a leader plays is that of teacher. For Senge, a leader is not the "authoritarian expert whose job it is to teach people [in the organization] the 'correct' view of reality," but the guide who pays "explicit attention to people's mental models" to help all in the organization understand and collaboratively influence that reality (Senge, 1990, p. 11). This concept may have special relevance for a Coordinator and teaching librarians who embrace constructivism, the educational theory in which "learning is enhanced when teachers pay attention to the knowledge and beliefs that learners bring" and harness this preexisting knowledge as an essential building block for the learners' construction of new knowledge (Bransford, Brown, & Cocking, 2000, p. 11).

The concept of "instructional leadership" comes from the literature of educational administration. Fowler and Walter (2003) introduce this model to the academic library setting, with compelling implications for an Instruction Coordinator. Instructional leadership encapsulates the role that an administrator "plays in helping to create a culture of instruction and assessment [. . .], placing student learning at the center of the instructional process, and fostering the professional growth of teachers as classroom instructors" (Fowler & Walter, 2003, p. 465). The instructional leader is a conduit between the organization (the library), its stakeholders (campus colleagues and the rest of the institution), and its broader context (academic librarianship and higher education). Saunders (2011) reviews the literature on "teacher-leaders" and makes a case for the role of teachers, not only as administrators, in instructional leadership. Through reflective practice, evidence-based decision-making, the willingness to take risks inside and outside of the classroom, and a propensity for collaboration, teacher-leaders (and by comparison, teacher-librarians) can effect change in their organizations (Saunders, 2011, pp. 266–67).

In fact, the Coordinator who comes from an instruction librarian background may be well positioned to lead through teaching. Mader (1996) notes the "natural affinity toward leadership positions" that many instruction librarians exhibit (p. 193). Instruction librarians "need to have vision to create a successful program," employ strong communication skills honed by "interacting with a variety of audiences," and they excel at collaborating and at "establish[ing] ongoing relationships" (Mader, 1996, p. 193). Above all, instruction librarians have a "strong philosophical vision of the role of libraries in the future," one that is centered on teaching and learning as a "vital link with our community of users" (Mader, 1996, p. 194). An Instruction Coordinator may already exhibit these essential dispositions before assuming a more formal leadership role.

Emotionally Intelligent Leadership

One of the foundational articulations of emotional intelligence, from Salovey and Mayer (1990), defines it as "the subset of social intelligence that involves the ability to monitor one's own and others' feelings and emotions, to discriminate among them, and to use this information to guide one's thinking and actions" (p. 189). Goleman (1995) defines emotional intelligence as "the capacity for recognizing our own feelings and those of others, for motivating ourselves, and for managing emotions well in ourselves and in our relationships" (p. 317). Some of the components included in emotional intelligence are self-awareness, empathy, social expertness, personal influence, and mastery of purpose and vision (Giesecke, 2007, p. 3).

Subsequent research, notably that of Goleman, Boyatzis, and McKee (2002), brings emotional intelligence into the workplace and into the management of organizations:

> Leadership is emotional; those leaders who excel in making their employees feel good are more successful in making them feel engaged, furthering the aims of the organization, and thus these leaders are more successful. [Goleman, Boyatzis, and McKee] offer a competency model consisting of capabilities grouped in four areas: self-awareness, self management, social awareness, and relationship management. (Ammons-Stephens, Cole, Jenkins-Gibbs, Riehle, & Weare Jr., 2009, p. 67)

It is from this perspective, in which emotional intelligence is deployed as a leadership tool, that an Instruction Coordinator might seek to expand their own capabilities. Emotional intelligence can be useful when providing feedback to staff (Giesecke, 2007, p. 5) or building a coaching or mentoring relationship (Alire, 2007, p. 101). For an Instruction Coordinator, or any leader, mastering one's own emotions, and being aware of how one "shows up" or presents oneself in the workplace, can also contribute to a feeling of stability among a team. The teaching and learning landscape in academic libraries is dynamic in and of itself; a steady, self-aware Instruction Coordinator can set a calm, measured, and resilient tone for an instruction team as they navigate change.

As Porter (2010) notes, the emotionally intelligent leader "learns how to work with and through others toward the desired outcome" (p. 199); this is a skill that is essential at all levels, not just for the library director. Kreitz (2009) conducted a survey of the Association of Research Library (ARL) directors and senior managers to understand which traits of emotional intelligence are most necessary and beneficial for directors and/or members of libraries' senior management teams. This study grew out of the literature of emotional intelligence and work teams, and as a corrective to a "monocentric focus on the top leader" (Kreitz, 2009, p. 533). Kreitz (2009) found that different aspects of emotional intelligence are salient for leaders at different organizational levels; for example, a director may be expected to *create* change (the end result), while the senior management team is tasked with actually *implementing* change (the process). In this case, the senior managers might use the emotional intelligence characteristics of empathy, respect for diverse experiences and viewpoints, and the ability to build consensus. Seen in this light, the Instruction Coordinator, regardless of their level in their organization's hierarchy, can contribute to the development of an emotionally intelligent workplace.

Of course, these are not the only leadership models that may be relevant to Instruction Coordinators. One model in particular, that of *servant leadership*, is espoused by many library leaders. Greenleaf (1977) conceives of servant leadership as the antithesis of a more traditional leadership model, in which the leader seeks to accumulate and wield power for their own gain. The servant-leader, on the other hand, views leadership as a form of service to the organization and to the individuals within it. Some of the core concepts of servant leadership, including empathy, are incorporated into this chapter, without explicit framing as characteristics of servant leadership. For an incisive critique of the gendered (feminized) nature of servant leadership, particularly within librarianship, see Richmond (2017).

CHARACTERISTICS AND DISPOSITIONS OF SUCCESSFUL INSTRUCTION COORDINATORS

Leadership models are just that: *models* of behavior and ways of thinking. It is helpful to have these concepts in one's coordinator toolkit, and essential to consider what these abstract concepts look like in action. The characteristics and dispositions of Instruction Coordinators are the bridge between leadership theories and practical applications in daily work.

The following is a non-exhaustive list of characteristics and dispositions that the author has found to be present in successful Instruction Coordinators, both through her own experience and through observations of others. These characteristics will be evident in all the discussions throughout this book. One important thing to remember is that, as with any career trajectory, values and dispositions change over time. Likewise, the skill sets and proficiencies desired by library administrators may not be explicitly characterized in the same way as the dispositions mentioned below. However, when applying or transitioning to a Coordinator role, one might think about how these dispositions can enhance or complement the strength areas asked for in job descriptions. In a study of job advertisements for library instruction roles, Gold and Grotti (2013) found that administrative skills, leadership skills, and subject expertise are among the most desired skills. While their study did not specifically focus on the skills required for Instruction Coordinators, connections can still be made. For example, dispositions such as empathy and holistic thinking pair well with administrative skills, which rely on activities "such as working well in a team and communicating instruction goals" (Gold & Grotti, 2013, p. 562).

Holistic Thinking

One of the most difficult characteristics to achieve, for anyone in a leadership role, is dealing with day-to-day issues while still focusing on how the program as a whole fits together. Instruction Coordinators need to focus on the macro and micro at the same time, remaining aware and cognizant of the big picture without losing sight of the people and practicalities that make up daily operations.

A concept from the literature of teaching and learning that speaks to this balance of the macro and micro is Parker Palmer's (1998) notion of "teaching from the microcosm." For Palmer, concerned with how to present the full scope of an academic discipline within the limits of time and the threat of cognitive overload, the microcosm approach is a synthesis of depth and breadth:

> Alone and together, guided by a teacher, they examine *this* grain of sand, and in the process, they learn the logic of the discipline, its rules of observation and interpretation, as well as some substantive facts. What they discover by examining this microcosm—then another, and another, and another—can eventually translate into literacy in the discipline at large. By diving deep into particularity, these students are developing an understanding of the whole. (Palmer, 1998, p. 123)

The holistically minded Instruction Coordinator can also think of an instruction program in terms of its "grains of sand." Each grain, such as a specific instruction session or an outreach message to faculty, can be seen as a microcosm of the overall program. If the big-picture mission of the instruction program is to contribute to and promote student learning, this mission should be visible in each and every instruction-related activity. When routine or mundane issues arise, maintaining a focus on these activities as a microcosm for the program can help the Coordinator make decisions and keep the program on course. Keeping in mind the question, "How does this serve the mission of our instruction program?" can be a powerful way to maintain alignment between particularity and holistic understanding.

Flexibility

Anyone who has dealt with scheduling a semester's worth of instruction sessions, fielding demanding requests from multiple faculty members in various departments, and accommodating librarians' diverse schedules knows the necessity of being flexible. For an Instruction Coordinator, this day-to-day flexibility exists alongside the big-picture perspective and may involve dealing with inconsistent support from upper-level administrators or shifting institutional priorities. Flexibility can also be seen in the willingness to shed preconceived ideas, to try new approaches, and to seize opportunities for strategic risks. This is an invaluable disposition when an environmental scan shows the need for change (see Chapter 2), or when an instruction program goes astray (see Chapter 8).

For example, when the ACRL *Framework* was adopted in 2016, some librarians expressed concern about implementing these new concepts, not out of an inherent dislike of change, but because of the massive investment of time, resources, and political capital that had gone into bringing the ACRL *Standards* (adopted in 2000) to their institutions. For librarians and Instruction Coordinators who had been successful in promoting an ACRL *Standards*-based view of information literacy on their campuses and in their accrediting bodies, the notion of switching to the ACRL *Framework* must have seemed like the undoing of more than a decade's worth of work and advocacy (for a deeper examination of this issue, see Chapter 4). These Instruction Coordinators faced a difficult choice: adapt to new professional practices while sacrificing hard-won local gains in teaching and learning, or hold fast to the ACRL *Standards* and risk drifting out of the mainstream of teaching and learning in academic librarianship.

Ultimately, the pro-ACRL *Standards* and the pro-ACRL *Framework* factions both expressed a desire for flexibility, either the flexibility of maintaining the ACRL *Standards* because of local usefulness, or the flexibility of embracing the ACRL *Framework* to transform pedagogical praxis. Flexibility, in this situation, means the ability to consider multiple perspectives, evaluate possibilities, and make informed decisions that may or may not lead to change.

Empathy

Empathy, an aspect of emotional intelligence, is one of the fundamental characteristics of a successful Instruction Coordinator. Doucette and Tolley (2017) note a need for co-worker relationships to be "founded on kindness, trust, and respect" (p. 170), and that demonstrating mindfulness and empathy can increase workplace civility. Each instruction librarian has their own responsibilities and associated challenges, which can sometimes outweigh or interfere with team goals. The Instruction Coordinator is often put in the position of navigating individuals' challenges while maintaining the team's focus; this requires compassion, patience, and empathy. It can be difficult to hold on to empathy when dealing with tough situations (personnel, programmatic, philosophical, or otherwise), but displaying "the emotional intelligence to remain open to different viewpoints, engage in real dialogue without blame, and clarify the issues at hand" (Doucette & Tolley, 2017, p. 181) goes a long way toward creating a respectful and high-performing instruction team.

While a crucial disposition, it is worth noting that empathy can have negative consequences and, at times, may contribute to burnout (discussed further in Chapters 8 and 9). Arellano Douglas and Gadsby (2017) find that Instruction Coordinators often feel the toll of the emotional labor that seems to be a natural part of leading in a service profession; direct supervisors, in particular, may feel this pull more acutely:

> one [Instruction Coordinator] who also served as a direct supervisor to their teaching team expressed a great deal of empathy and compassion for new librarians in the form of frequent check-ins, an open door policy, and extensive mentoring. This is an all-give and no-take situation, that although ultimately rewarding, takes a great deal more time and effort than supervising established professionals. (p. 270)

An excess of empathy from the manager or leader can also limit the growth of individuals and the overall effectiveness of the team. Scott (2017) proposes the concept of "ruinous empathy," a state in which a manager, concerned for the emotional well-being of a team member, shields the individual from genuine feedback and constructive criticism. Consider a teaching librarian who struggles with public speaking; a manager can empathize with feelings of anxiety when speaking to groups but would do a disservice to the librarian by offering false praise or suggesting that the ability to speak confidently in the classroom is unimportant for effective teaching. This empathy comes from a place of caring, but it becomes "ruinous" when it treats the individual as too fragile to handle the challenging questions and honest coaching that are often necessary to spur development. Empathy is essential for an Instruction Coordinator, but as with many aspects of leadership, it requires balance.

Toughness

Instruction Coordinators must exhibit a certain amount of "toughness" to maintain equilibrium among the instruction team and keep the program moving forward. Whether this means coaching reluctant librarians to improve their teaching skills or addressing interpersonal or institutional challenges,

Instruction Coordinators need to be prepared to make, or at least advocate for, hard decisions that are unlikely to satisfy all of their colleagues.

One facet of toughness is the ability to address conflict in a productive manner. Plocharczyk (2007) notes that "conflict is both inevitable and necessary for continuous growth and change within the work environment" (p. 98). Even though libraries are likely to aspire to consensus (Krautter, 2013), many organizational structures promote the uneven spread of information across departments (Pettas & Gilliland, 1992) or cause role ambiguity to flourish (Plocharczyk, 2007). Krautter (2013) proposes the role of "devil's advocate" as a mediator in conflict situations: "The devil's advocate can be a potentially valuable factor in promoting an atmosphere of openness and creative problem solving without increasing unproductive conflict" (p. 9). In a conflict of ideas, an Instruction Coordinator can exhibit toughness, and fairness, by helping participants to explore multiple perspectives without succumbing to negativity or passive-aggressive avoidance.

**Textbox 1.1. Put It in Practice:
Are You an Intentional Instruction Coordinator?**
Answer these questions to find out!

- Do you take time to do strategic planning or goal setting for your instruction program?

  - Yes
  - Sometimes
  - No

- Do you take time to set goals for yourself and plan for your own professional and personal development?

  - Yes
  - Sometimes
  - No

- Do you build in time for reflection on your own work as an Instruction Coordinator?

  - Yes
  - Sometimes
  - No

- Do you have consistent check-ins with your manager/supervisor?

- Yes
- Sometimes
- No

- Do you provide regular feedback to the librarians and staff you coordinate?

  - Yes
  - Sometimes
  - No

- Do you actively seek feedback from the librarians and staff you coordinate?

  - Yes
  - Sometimes
  - No

- If you don't have well-defined instructional roles in your library, do you assign classes to others before taking on most of the teaching load yourself?

  - Yes
  - Sometimes
  - No

- When work piles up, do you take it in stride instead of getting frustrated?

  - Yes
  - Sometimes
  - No

Did you mostly answer *yes*? You are doing great! It can be difficult to remain intentional in your practice, but you seem to have developed good habits—stick with it! Were you answers mostly *sometimes*? You might want to begin building (and maintaining) regular practices that allow you to slow down and reflect, as well as create opportunities for more open communication—both for yourself and your colleagues. If you answered mostly *no*, then it would likely benefit you to take a moment to think about why. Try to get to the root of what's holding you back, either consciously or subconsciously. Are there small actions or behaviors you can change, which might turn into regular habits? If

> you had an even mix of responses, that's perfectly normal; it is very easy to get caught up in day-to-day work, which may mean falling back on comfortable habits. Celebrate the work you do, and don't get discouraged!

Intentionality

Intentionality encompasses all the preceding traits. It combines big-picture thinking, adaptability, empathy, compassion, and the willingness to address difficult challenges. In the context of teaching librarians, Booth (2011) defines intentionality as:

> constructive self-awareness in teaching. Intentional instructors do more than communicate well or design strong assignments; they methodically consider the impact their actions have on learners, understand the knowledge they possess, use evidence to support the strategies they select, and strive to improve their effectiveness over time. (p. 17)

Instruction Coordinators can apply this disposition of intentionality to their own work as well. An intentional Instruction Coordinator knows that "there is always more to learn" (Grassian & Kaplowitz, 2005, p. 21). This learning happens on several levels: in the Coordinator's careful consideration of a variety of points of view and experiences, in their attention to their own professional development, and in their commitment to fostering "an atmosphere in which new ideas and approaches can bubble to the surface" (Grassian & Kaplowitz, 2005, p. 22). At the heart of intentionality is reflection, which "invites us to step back and take stock of what we're doing and why" (Jacobs, 2016, p. 16). Through reflection, an Instruction Coordinator can "move closer to living [their] intentions" while "learning from [their] experiences" (Giesecke, 2007, p. 6).

Beyond this individual, personal reflection, an Instruction Coordinator can bring intentionality to their team and their organization. Kubicek (2012) asserts that leaders should be intentional with time, with "improving the levels of leadership," with organizational and team development, and one's own personal growth (p. 40). Cultivation of a leadership mindset is not something that happens immediately; rather, it requires care, attention, and a good deal of practice:

> Intentional Leadership is a process like apprenticeship. We must know what we are trying to raise up and reproduce. It starts with a mind-set change and is structured through a plan made up of trade-up moments. It is a great culture builder and the most effective way we have seen for building a dynamic culture of growth. (Kubicek, 2012, p. 43)

Systems thinking, as described by Senge (1990), is a fitting complement to intentionality. This entails breaking out of "events and reactiveness," or a mindset of moving "from crisis to crisis," to see the underlying structures, interconnected relationships, and emerging trends that affect an organization (Senge, 1990, p. 16). The intentional Instruction Coordinator can use a systems thinking approach to avoid implementing quick fixes that address symptoms, not causes, in the same way that they would incorporate reflection into their personal practice to better understand their own experiences, strengths, and areas for growth.

EMBRACING INTENTIONALITY AS AN INSTRUCTION COORDINATOR

The Instruction Coordinator role varies among institutions, and Coordinators themselves come to their roles with different experiences, approaches, and strengths. Many sections throughout this book will return to the idea of *intentionality* as a common thread among leaders of successful academic library instruction programs. Intentionality is a model for leadership, as well as a disposition and a set of practices. While the professional twists and turns of each Instruction Coordinator and the contours of each instruction program differ, the Coordinator is in a position to reflect on their library and their institution, carefully build a program, foster a robust culture of teaching and learning, and continually evaluate and adapt their instruction program. All this comes from intention, not happenstance.

The chapters that follow recommend strategies to assist Instruction Coordinators in developing their programs, their relationships with stakeholders, their instructional team, and themselves in ways that are grounded in scholarship, best practices, and, above all, leadership that is reflective and intentional.

NOTE

1. Prior to 2017, this document was called the *Standards for Proficiencies for Instruction Librarians and Coordinators*; it influenced many job descriptions and guided new and seasoned Instruction Coordinators in their roles.

Chapter Two

Taking Stock of an Instruction Program

YOU'RE IN CHARGE OF AN INSTRUCTION PROGRAM. NOW WHAT?

The previous chapter introduced the Instruction Coordinator role as it relates to leading a teaching and learning program: who is considered an Instruction Coordinator? What do they do, and how do they mark their successes? Just as there is no "one size fits all" for the Instruction Coordinator role, academic library instruction programs come in all shapes and sizes.

INSTRUCTION PROGRAM MAKEUP

Those in charge might find themselves leading a large instruction program in which they do not manage any other staff; or directing a program in which they supervise all, or some of, the teaching librarians; or leading a program of one: made up only of themselves! Even within medium-sized instruction programs, there are often distinctions as to how active librarians are in terms of their teaching load and/or other responsibilities, which could range from research data support to reference work to collection development. Instruction programs that rely on the liaison model fall into this category; some liaison models distribute teaching load by department, whereas some divide up instruction responsibilities by discipline or "type" (e.g., undergraduate/graduate/professional or general education/upper level). Liaison models have seen rapid changes over the last several decades, moving from a more traditional model to a more "engaged" philosophy, with many applying significant emphasis on teaching partnerships (Jaguszewski & Williams, 2013; Kenney, 2014). Furthermore, some instruction programs are more formal, with defined roles, while some programs are fairly informal and ad hoc. An instruction program may rely mostly on a course-integrated model for academic departments, while still not having a cohesive plan for instruction.

Each organizational scenario poses its own challenges and benefits, many of which will be explored throughout this book. Despite the size or makeup, however, all the aforementioned program categories do indeed constitute an instruction program, and readers are encouraged to reflect on their own institutional scenario as they move through this book. Many of the suggestions and strategies can be adapted for any size and type of academic library instruction program, whether formal or informal.

For new Instruction Coordinators, or even for those that have been in their positions for a significant length of time, it is important to take stock of one's environment; this is a healthy and necessary activity for a leader in any organization. While this scrutiny can (and should!) be internal, as discussed in Chapter 1, it is crucial for anyone leading an instruction program to also turn that scrutiny outward, analyzing the landscape of both the library and the larger institution. This chapter provides strategies for not only identifying the type of instruction program one finds themselves leading, but also engages readers in an exploration of how that program fits into the larger library organization. Finally, continuing outward, the chapter will conclude with a discussion regarding how the teaching and learning culture on campus, in addition to institutional priorities, can affect and guide a library's instruction program.

GATHERING THE DATA

An environmental scan can be accomplished through a variety of methods: data collection (surveys, focus groups, interviews, etc.), external and internal benchmarks, a review of existing literature and institutional documents, and, of course, conversations with faculty and administrators. Perhaps most importantly, the Coordinator does not have to be the sole means of gathering this information; in fact, deploying librarians in the teaching and learning program to help take stock is a great way to promote buy-in and leverage librarians' existing relationships with departments and stakeholders. Additionally, librarians may have already collected many of the program and course-specific details. It would also be beneficial to talk to library administrators or others that may have documentation from campus conversations related to strategic planning or curricular decisions.

SURVEYING THE LANDSCAPE . . . IN THE LIBRARY

The first step in taking stock of one's instruction program is to perform an audit of current efforts. When leading a teaching and learning program, it can be easy to get lost in the details of daily work and the logistics of making sure everything is getting accomplished. However, to begin any kind of strategic planning and visioning for a program (discussed in more detail in Chapters 3 and 5), it is necessary to first objectively examine the environment in which the instruction program operates. Bruch and Wilkinson (2012) call this environmental scan "surveying terrain" and recommend a holistic look at the culture, structure, and interpersonal aspects of library instruction. In other words, who makes up a program? What is the focus of the program? What resources are available (or lacking) to both the Coordinator and the instruction program in general?

The People

Examining the people that make up an instruction program will help provide context and ground further analysis of the program. Who participates in the library's teaching program? Who are the primary stakeholders in the library? The answer will likely vary depending on the institutional makeup, as described earlier, but this is the time to take an audit of who is responsible for most library instruction and how much of their jobs are devoted to teaching.

While it can be difficult to determine an average percentage of time librarians spend on teaching, particularly if there are blurred lines between classroom teaching and reference or research consultations, some extrapolations may help provide at least an estimate of instruction loads. For example, in a study of information literacy librarians, Seymour (2012) found that "approximately 50% of [respondents'] time is spent providing reference assistance and it isn't possible to differentiate between reference and instructional services" (p. 53). Tracking time spent on noncredit course teaching (e.g., course-integrated sessions, workshops) is particularly difficult, as it looks a little different for each librarian and is harder to calculate consistently. Coordinators may find it helpful to create a survey or even an informal poll to track the time librarians spend in the classroom, the time spent on preparing for a class (or other pedagogical activities, such as creating assessments), and the amount of nondirectional reference/research consultation appointments. Making these distinctions can help delineate between the reality and the perception of time spent on teaching activities. Other strategies for analyzing teaching time and efforts across an instruction program include an examination of statistics (such as the number of sessions taught divided by number of librarian instructors) or calculating the percentage of teaching within a librarians' workload (i.e., Is the number accurate based on their job description or contract? Has the percentage been inflated or grown over time?). A thorough examination of teaching capacity can also provide more insight into scaling up a program, and likely will impact requests for and allocations of resources (more on this next).

Whether or not librarians see themselves as teachers has an impact on the instruction program; if librarians embrace their teaching role, this attitude is likely to bolster a program, no matter how small. On the other hand, if librarians do not see themselves as "teachers," it can be difficult to articulate the library's instructional efforts as true contributions to teaching and learning (both in the library and on campus). Julien and Pecoskie (2009) note that,

> In spite of the fact that librarians' instructional work is important and increasingly central to the activities of academic librarians, previous research shows some ambivalence about instructional roles on the part of some library staff. Some librarians remain unconvinced of the value of information literacy instruction, some feel unprepared for instructional roles, and some express hostility towards the instructional expectations they feel towards the students they teach and towards the teaching faculty on campuses. (p. 149)

Conflicting priorities, whether due to the nature of teaching librarians' jobs, contradictory pedagogical goals or values, personal preferences for teaching, or unmet cultural expectations can all affect the success of an instruction program. Chapter 3 goes into more detail on the topic of establishing a culture of teaching within the library, while addressing some of these issues.

The Focus

Although not updated since the adoption of ACRL *Framework* (2015), the Association of College and Research Libraries' (ACRL) *Guidelines for Instruction Programs in Academic Libraries* (2011) provides helpful parameters for both examining and contextualizing an instruction program. Among the suggested areas of focus are:

Statement of Purpose

Does the instruction program have an established (and documented) mission or vision statement or program goals? Or are the goals implied? This answer may differ depending on how well established or formal or informal an instruction program is. Chapter 5 goes into more detail about writing an instruction program statement, but at the beginning stages of taking stock of one's instruction program, it can be useful to deploy an environmental scan to determine if there are any stated or implicit teaching and learning goals in the library as a whole.

Content of Instruction

The "content" of the teaching efforts not only influences student learning assessment efforts but also greatly impacts alignment to both national information literacy standards and institutional priorities. As noted next, the connection to the institution is a crucial component when situating an instruction program within campus teaching and learning environments, and is an important tool for marketing and promoting the library's instruction efforts.

Modes of Instruction

What are the current teaching efforts? Are librarians mostly engaging in one-shot instruction? Is information literacy integrated into the curriculum? How (if at all) does the university's general education program impact the library's instructional efforts? Is teaching provided mostly in-person, online (synchronously or asynchronously), or as a hybrid? Answers to these questions provide a baseline for the current efforts as well as help the Coordinator identify areas in which more resources are needed.

Program Structures

According to the ACRL *Guidelines* (2011) document:

> Instruction programs should identify curricular and academic programs already in place or under development who will support evolving approaches to information literacy programming. Instruction librarians themselves should also seek opportunities for collaborative engagement in new institutional initiatives and redesigned curricula that allow for a deeper interplay between the library's instruction program and the total campus learning environment. (ACRL, 2011)

Recognizing how the instruction program fits into the larger *library* priorities and goals is a good first step to aligning the library's teaching and learning efforts to those happening on campus.

Evaluation and Assessment

Finally, it is crucial to develop a plan for assessing the program's success. While not altogether separate, this assessment goes beyond just student learning assessment and should be influenced by the program's statement of purpose. This will be explored further in Chapter 7, which goes into more depth on assessing instruction programs.

Again, since every instruction program is unique, this environmental scan will look different from program to program—there is no one "perfect" model of an instruction program's makeup; rather, Coordinators should explore each of the areas with a holistic view of the overall instruction program. This examination may also provide the impetus to critically examine the way teaching has traditionally been accomplished and whether or not this will still be an effective way of structuring the instruction program. As Jaguszewski and Williams (2013) note,

> programmatic efforts with information literacy have been too narrowly defined. It is not unusual for libraries to focus on freshman writing programs and a series of "one-shot" or invited guest lectures in individual courses [. . .] traditional one-shot, in-person instructional sessions can vary in quality [. . .] and they neither scale well nor do they necessarily address broader curricular goals. (p. 6)

One-shot, synchronous instruction has been the foundation of many instruction programs, due in part to factors relating to the size of the library instruction department, demand for instruction, and more. A good rule for library instruction program development (or revision) is to have an honest assessment of what teaching has looked like in the past and what impact that may have on current and future efforts. Are students still learning in the same way? Has the content of the instruction changed? Perhaps there are other, better ways to deliver instruction; for example, through asynchronous tutorials, live webinars, or on-demand workshops. This assessment can be difficult, particularly if it means changing the very focus of the instruction program, but when doing this type of environmental scanning, a Coordinator should be open to the idea of realignment.

The Resources

The ACRL *Guidelines* (2011) also suggests auditing an instruction program for auxiliary factors, such as instructional spaces, IT support, financial resources (for training, program evaluation, etc.), and support for pedagogical training of teaching librarians (will this happen in-house or are external training opportunities required?). An environmental scan of existing resources related to technology and space benchmarked to other similarly sized programs can be used to petition library (and sometimes campus) administrators for additional financial support and, in some cases, personnel.

Coordinators should also take stock of the climate within their organization; in particular, the administrative support for teaching and learning in the libraries. Library administrative support (or lack thereof) is an important indicator of the work that will need to be done in instruction program landscaping. In other words, is teaching viewed as a priority? How does it fit within the greater library's goals, objectives, and mission? Are teaching and assessment part of librarians' job descriptions and expectations? Finally, what does support look like? The perception of administrative support may not always match up with the realities and expectations of teaching librarians. For example, a conversation with administrators may reveal that while they indicate support of librarians' teaching activities, they may also have unrealistic expectations for teaching load and/or misconceptions about librarian/faculty partnerships. On the other hand, the library's administration may be particularly supportive of the instruction program, providing budgets for professional development or supplies, building in time for librarians' teaching prep, or through other actions. The Instruction Coordinator will need to have a clear picture of the level of support (both perceived and actual) from above to proceed with planning.

Regardless of how the library's administration prioritizes the instruction program, the views of librarians that participate in the program can go a long way in shaping attitudes. In a study of academic instruction librarians, Seymour (2012) found that librarians felt that the library "is part of an educational culture with the mission to provide instruction and support for learning throughout the institution" (p. 66). Librarians' attitudes toward teaching, and the connection to their pedagogical skill development, is further explored in Chapter 3.

SURVEYING THE LANDSCAPE... ON CAMPUS

When taking stock of the teaching and learning landscape on campus, one strategy is to follow the journalistic five Ws (plus that additional H): who, what, when where, why, and how (see Textbox 2.1).

Textbox 2.1. Put It in Practice: The Five Ws Campus Scan

WHO

- Who are your campus stakeholders? Who has the most to gain from supporting the library's instruction efforts (e.g., academic program coordinators, deans or administrators involved in accreditation, faculty, students, advisors)?
- Who is doing most of the teaching on campus (e.g., adjuncts, tenured faculty, graduate students, lecturers)?
- Who will your librarians partner with and what are their shared priorities?

WHAT

- What is the teaching and learning culture on campus?
- What are your institution's priorities (stated or undefined) and focus on teaching and/or research?
- What are faculty views of librarians as teachers?

WHEN

- When are librarians teaching? Are they mostly teaching one-shot sessions early in the semester? Are they embedded in programs and providing instructional support throughout the term?

WHERE

- Where is teaching happening (e.g., online, in physical classrooms, or a hybrid model)?
- Where do conversations relating to pedagogy happen on campus? Does your campus have a teaching center or faculty development program?

WHY

- Why do faculty members partner (or decline to partner) with librarians? Can you identify the level of faculty respect for library instruction, librarians as teaching partners, and/or the library as leader of teaching efforts on campus?

HOW

- How can you tie into institutional goals?
- How does information literacy fit into institutional or program accreditation requirements?

This process can provide a framework for identifying the context in which the instruction program is situated. It may be helpful for the Coordinator to reflect on these questions individually first, and then with the teaching librarians to identify their own gaps in knowledge. This is particularly helpful for new Coordinators who have less awareness of campus culture. The answers to the questions in Textbox 2.1 can help guide next steps, and can also be used as a conversation starter when talking with teaching librarians, library administration, and/or campus stakeholders (Harland, Stewart, & Bruce, 2018), and to align the program's priorities and goals to larger library or campus goals.

Institutional Teaching Culture

The culture question is a big one. What exactly *is* the institutional teaching and learning culture? The answer to this can greatly impact the success of a library instruction program. For example, is there a stated commitment to teaching and learning? If so, it helps to identify the guiding factors of this commitment. Does accreditation guide the commitment? Is it part of the university's mission or vision? A stated commitment to student learning can be reflected in the institutional culture, but an "official" written affirmation toward teaching and learning is not necessarily required to result in a rich commitment to teaching on campus. This commitment to teaching may be more ad hoc in nature and be evidenced by a strong and active center for teaching or even just by innovative classroom partnerships. Regardless of the way it is communicated or the formality of the institution's commitment to teaching and learning, it is important to identify the culture on campus to situate the library's instruction program within that culture and to identify potential roadblocks or pushback.

Analyzing librarian and faculty teaching relationships can go a long way in uncovering campus commitment to the library's teaching efforts. While challenges are likely, due to campus hierarchies and power structures (Julien & Pecoskie, 2009), it is even more likely that there are very successful library-faculty partnerships. To maintain perspective, the Instruction Coordinator should take a holistic view of these relationships and look for trends across the instruction program rather than isolating individual challenges or beneficial interactions. As Mallon (2018) notes,

> librarian liaisons bring a number of beneficial roles to the campus teaching team:
>
> - Individual research consultations with students support deeper level learning and provide visibility for librarians;
> - Liaisons are known in their departments for their subject expertise; many have advanced degrees and/or prior work experience to support this;
> - Liaisons consistently demonstrate a willingness to collaborate across disciplinary and geographical boundaries; and
> - Liaisons establish successful co-curricular relationships, and often have more developed connections with academic departments that some academic departments may not have cultivated. (p. 117)

Identifying Institutional Priorities

There are several methods by which librarians can align their instruction program with the institution to meet accreditation requirements and to support and further the institution's strategic initiatives.

Curriculum Mapping

One specific strategy for tying an instruction program's goals/mission to institutional priorities is through the practice of curriculum mapping. This is an effective way to make visual connections between the program curriculum and information literacy skills. The National Institute for Learning Outcomes Assessment (2018) notes that mapping "is a key strategy for examining the role of different elements of learning environments as they build towards shared learning outcomes as well as to better understand where to assess and document learning" (p. 3). It can also be a useful exercise for a Coordinator to engage their teaching librarians in mapping instruction program outcomes to departmental and university program outcomes (both curricular and co-curricular). According to Bruch and Wilkinson (2012),

> Ideal curricula integration includes objective measures such as meaningful learning outcomes in many (or most) campus disciplines or programs, or the adoption and completion of program goals at the institutional level, in addition to a group of librarians willing to experiment with pedagogy and assessment in order to evolve and improve their teaching methods. Changing a culture on this frontier requires years of political persuasion both within and outside of the library environment and simultaneously by cultivating respect of academic librarian knowledge, integrating librarians into the classroom, and compelling departmental ownership of curriculum reform and rewarding innovative and authentic teaching. (pp. 10–11)

Curriculum mapping provides a logical space for not only institutional alignment of information literacy skills, but also provides a path for communicating the instruction program's goals and mission. Curriculum mapping can also be used to strategically promote (and advocate) an instruction program to the broader campus (see Chapter 6).

Accreditation

When taking stock of the campus landscape related to teaching and learning, particularly when identifying how and where an instruction program fits in, looking at accreditation efforts is a logical start: "thinking beyond individual courses, libraries can be instrumental in helping a university (both at the microprogram level and the macro-institutional level) demonstrate achievement of learning standards required for accreditation" (Mallon, 2018, p. 123).

Curriculum mapping and accreditation can also go hand in hand; Messersmith (2015) notes that one of the ways curriculum mapping provides value is that it can provide more accountability for the student learning process, an important aspect of many accreditation requirements. This can serve as the jumping-off point for librarian partnerships with faculty and administrators: "campus-wide discussions and initiatives centered around [accreditation] stimulate collaboration among interdisciplinary faculty who would not otherwise meet outside of an established structure" (Messersmith, 2015, para. 21).

Strategic Plans

Participating in departmental strategic planning efforts "provides an additional avenue for librarians to engage in the teaching and learning process" (Mallon, 2018, p. 117). Connecting to institutional strategic plans related to teaching and learning or information and digital literacies is a logical starting point; libraries are accustomed to making interdisciplinary connections and showcasing the value of the library to a variety of campus activities and initiatives. This same approach can be used for instruction programs. Kenney (2014) asserts that libraries should "look at the indicators that are motivating your university, not your library" (p. 6), as a reminder for focusing efforts outward. When developing instruction program outcomes and curriculum alignment, cross-walking to strategic plans or other guiding documents will better position instruction program Coordinators for promoting the value and necessity of the library in positively impacting student learning.

AFTER THE SURVEY: NEXT STEPS

Needs Analysis

After gathering the initial data, Coordinators are ready to move on to program development. One way to use this data is by conducting a needs analysis, defined by Witkin and Altschuld (1995) as: "a systematic set of procedures undertaken for the purpose of setting priorities and making decisions about a program or organizational improvement and allocation of resources. The priorities are based on identified needs" (p. 4). Identifying and categorizing the needs of the different stakeholders will provide a logical step forward: where are the gaps? Which needs are already being met (and which ones are not)?

A needs analysis can also provide fodder for developing the structure and outcomes of an instruction program; a needs assessment is a data-driven way to find out about faculty misconceptions related to information literacy and student learning gaps (Pemberton, 2010) as well as uneven representation of information literacy skills across the curriculum (Messersmith, 2015).

Moving Forward

The gaps and weak points identified in the needs analysis should guide the momentum and development of not only the program structure but also the relationships that need to be cultivated, as well as shaping the general culture related to teaching and learning within the instruction program itself. This may mean looking beyond the library and using other, similar campus entities (such as academic affairs, advising, or various research centers) to help guide and influence program development.

The data-gathering phase ("taking stock," as it is termed in this chapter), is the embodiment of the "pre-assessment" phase of the needs analysis process (Witkin & Altschuld, 1995); the subsequent phases of "assessment" and "post-assessment" are incorporated throughout the remainder of the book; more details on assessing an instruction program are covered in Chapter 7, and Chapter 8 details what happens if (or perhaps *when*), the program is not working as it was intended. This chapter has provided the foundation for an Instruction Coordinator to take stock of both the library and the university's landscapes. This is, of course, a first step but also a step that may need to be revisited over time. Administrators will change, new strategic plans will be adopted, and librarians will join or leave the instruction team. These types of changes are inevitable, but can also serve as catalysts to reexamine and adapt the focus of an instruction program. The next several chapters will continue to further explore the areas introduced in this chapter, with an eye toward enhanced program development. Chapter 3, for example, tackles the need to create a culture of instruction in the library; depending on what the environmental scan revealed about the "people" involved in the teaching and learning program, further developing a sense of community within the program will build upon librarians' teaching practices and create a more holistic approach to the library's instructional efforts. Chapter 4 examines the ACRL *Framework* as a possible document for guiding the program's overall structure. However, to further underscore the need for institutional alignment, as discussed earlier, the authors also encourage readers to determine whether or not the ACRL *Framework* fits into an institution's teaching culture and priorities.

Chapter Three

Creating a Culture of Teaching and Learning in the Library

IDENTIFYING AND DEFINING CULTURE

The idea of "culture" in libraries is often used in many contexts to indicate shared values or to drive the work of the academic library: library administrators attempt to create a *culture of assessment*, library staff are encouraged to participate in a *culture of innovation*, and *workplace culture* is examined and updated through new workflows or policies. But what about a culture of teaching? The question is one that many Coordinators of teaching and learning programs must consider, particularly as they work to both articulate and further the mission and vision of the library's instruction program (this is especially relevant to the development of the instruction program statement, which is discussed in further detail in Chapter 5). The teaching and learning culture is dependent on many factors, including overall library culture, but Coordinators are in a unique position to help define and influence the overall "vibe" of the instruction program. As Walter (2015) notes, many academic libraries do indeed view "the idea of a 'culture of teaching' as critical to any departmental or institutional attempt to improve the quality of instructional performance" (p. 366). Building and sustaining an environment that encourages curiosity, innovation, and risk-taking is key to securing buy-in from teaching librarians and for advocating the library's role in teaching and learning across campus.

DEVELOPING A CULTURE OF TEACHING AND LEARNING

Hutchings (1996) defines a teaching and learning culture as "one in which teaching and learning are the subject of sustained, public attention and inquiry, and where members of the academic community take seriously their shared responsibility for ensuring and improving the quality of the educational experience" (p. 4). So how does one begin creating this culture? Simply encouraging and fostering discussions about teaching and learning is one logical, and low threshold, way to begin. Hutchings (1996) recommends starting by increasing the dialogue about teaching and learning:

> Conversation about teaching and learning needs to increase, but it also needs to be more informed, more information-based. (Indeed, it might be argued that more talk without better information will be detrimental, simply digging us deeper into current quagmires and misunderstandings.) What's needed are strategies for and habits of inquiry into our work as educators—ways of asking what, as a consequence of the educational experiences we provide, our students know and can do. (p. 6)

While engaging librarians in conversations about student learning is an important component, and is discussed at length in this book, this chapter focuses on the need to develop academic librarians' teacher identity to build and sustain a culture of teaching and learning in the library; so, in this context, the "students" Hutchings refers to are instruction librarians.

If the instruction librarians are to be considered essential stakeholders in creating a culture of teaching, then who should lead them in these conversations? Sonntag (2007) argues that while one of the most important aspects of successful information literacy teaching programs is the librarians, one cannot overlook the criticality of the Instruction Coordinator: "the coordinator must be a coach, mentor, teacher, friend, and fan club to the instruction team, creating and nurturing a strong ethos [. . .] part of the learning process [for librarians] is thinking systematically about pedagogical practice and learning from experience" (p. 139). By fostering a culture of teaching, and learning about teaching, Instruction Coordinators can play the role of the coach and aid in the success of individual librarians' pedagogical development as well as the instruction program as a whole. The same holds true for anyone leading a teaching and learning program (no matter the size or organization of that program), not just those with the title of "Coordinator" or "Director." These leaders are in an important position to help guide and support teaching librarians by creating a teaching culture that supports and rewards innovation and curiosity:

> Leaders often have a space of action where it is possible to influence [. . .] inhibiting structures. In an organisation characterised by internal responsive-

ness, leaders must be sensitive to the needs of teachers and change regulations when necessary in order to support and promote development. This requires methods by which leaders develop their capacity to listen to the experiences of teachers and also their ability to take appropriate measures in terms of supporting teaching and learning development. This is important for all the efforts made by individual academic teachers to reach their full potential in terms of collaboration and mutual support. (Mårtensson, Roxå, & Olsson, 2011, p. 59)

In addition to pedagogical and programmatic development, it is also important for instruction program leaders to assess institutional culture. As Kustra et al. (2014) note,

The purpose of developing and identifying indicators of institutional teaching culture is to promote, encourage, and contribute to quality teaching. An effective institutional teaching culture recognizes the importance of teaching, constructively assesses teaching, engages various stakeholders and resources, and supports teacher development. (p. 7)

As introduced in the previous chapter, the extent to which the institution's culture is focused on teaching and learning impacts many factors for the library's instruction program, including buy-in from faculty for curriculum-integrated information literacy, acceptance of the library's role in student learning, and acknowledgment of librarians as partners in teaching. Mader and Gibson (2019) found that campus Centers for Teaching and Learning are a logical place to start for identifying institutional culture in this area because the centers are often seen as "hubs [. . .] where faculty can engage in pedagogical experimentation, in conversations with colleagues about that experimentation, and where they can showcase their learning about pedagogy" (p. 791).

Librarians are in an extremely good position to help shape those conversations and are logical partners in advancing pedagogy in the institution (Mader & Gibson, 2019). But are librarians ready and willing to take on that role? As noted, there needs to be a strong foundation for a teaching and learning culture; an equally crucial component is the role of librarians and the importance of acknowledging their identity as teachers in helping shape this culture in the library and on campus.

COORDINATING "LIBRARIANS THAT TEACH"

Most formalized instruction programs (particularly liaison-centric programs) are typically made up of librarians whose primary or secondary job responsibilities include a fair amount of teaching. However, these programs often fail to provide oversight of librarians whose jobs may include only tertiary teaching responsibilities, such as those in scholarly communications or technical services roles (occasionally referred to as "functional" liaisons). These librarians may teach, but perhaps not regularly or in any kind of formal or programmatic way. While the Instruction Coordinator may not be responsible for overseeing or directing these librarians' teaching, there are still many opportunities to integrate their work into the teaching goals and mission of the library. Providing opportunities for *all* librarians that have instructional roles to share resources, benefit from professional development, and participate in discussions related to teaching, goes a long way toward establishing and maintaining a culture of teaching that is pervasive throughout the library.

Given that some liaison librarians may feel that there are too many "hats" to juggle in addition to a heavy teaching load, some libraries have elected to organize public services librarians by more job-specific roles, such as collection development and management, digital scholarship and scholarly communications, or teaching and information literacy instruction (Jaguszewski & Williams, 2013). This organization can help create more of a community and shared values among librarians that have teaching as a primary role, but there might still be a disconnect or lack of participation by librarians in other areas that may have smaller teaching roles.

Teaching Identities

Although instruction librarians spend a considerable amount of time reflecting on teaching practices to improve instruction, they rarely have time, or in some cases, the pedagogical background and vocabulary, to reflect on their own *identity* as an authentic teacher (Cranton, 2001; Donovan, 2009; Evans, 2007; Laursen, 2005). Encouraging librarians to examine and reflect on their role in the classroom can also help facilitate and strengthen a library's teaching culture. Donovan (2009) asserts that:

> for teaching to be memorable and meaningful, it must come from the true self and from a willingness to share the beliefs, values, and perspectives that shape it. Espousing this type of behavior in ourselves will encourage our learners to examine what shapes their identity, thereby creating opportunities for learning surrounding the questions and curiosities that arise as a result of self-disclosure, self-awareness, and self-examination. (para. 12)

Encouraging instruction librarians to focus on their inner belief system and their sense of "self" when it comes to their identity as a teacher can also go a long way in helping the Coordinator articulate the goals and purpose of the overarching program, as well as the library's role in teaching and learning.

Administering a teaching identity survey is one way of helping librarians categorize the work they do, providing shared language that can be useful in developing a teaching culture. Several possibilities of diagnostic tools include:

- Grasha-Riechmann Teaching Style Survey, http://longleaf.net/teachingstyle.html
- Teaching Perspectives Inventory, http://www.teachingperspectives.com/tpi/

Using an instrument from outside of libraries will provide more validity to aid librarians in recognizing that teachers are teachers, regardless of the departments they work in (e.g., libraries or academic/disciplinary departments).

Exploration of the "act" of teaching is another way to help librarians relate the work they do to those of their disciplinary counterparts:

> [teaching] includes a broad vision of disciplinary questions and methods; it includes the capacity to plan and design activities that implement the vision; it includes the interactions that require particular skills and result in both expected and unexpected results; it includes certain outcomes from that complex process, and those outcomes necessitate some kind of analysis. (Bass, 1999, p. 2)

A concept related to the act of teaching (which connects to a teacher's identity) is that of an intentional unpredictability and fondness for questioning, as articulated by Bass and Eynon (1998). The Scholarship of Teaching and Learning (discussed in more detail in Chapter 4, in the context of librarians as teachers and researchers; see also Mårtensson, Roxå, & Olsson [2011]), is founded on the idea of asking questions (rather than specifically seeking answers), such as:

- What are your objectives for introducing work with technologies into your class?
- What pedagogical problems are you trying to solve?
- What are you able to do now that you couldn't do before? What is being gained? What are the trade-offs? What do you have to give up or change? Where is the "overhead"?
- What about particular activities most surprised you? What most frustrated you? (Bass & Eynon, 1998, p. 13).

Although most often used in student learning or classroom contexts, these questions can be applied to librarians' pedagogical practice (see the Hutchings [1996] discussion from earlier). It can be confusing and it can be messy, but questioning and investigating is an excellent way to push the boundaries of defining a culture of teaching and learning.

Providing librarians (and other colleagues) with the opportunity to individually reflect on their role as a teacher as well as creating a space for dialogue to articulate and expand on this reflection as a group will go a long way in helping to foster the kind of teaching and learning culture that provides structure and purpose for a library's instruction program. The following section discusses using the approach of Communities of Practice as a catalyst for discussing librarians' teacher identity and fostering a culture of teaching and learning in libraries.

COMMUNITIES OF PRACTICE

Lave and Wenger (1991) describe Communities of Practice as "groups of people who share a concern or a passion for something they do and learn how to do it better as they interact regularly." Communities of Practice (CoP) are fairly common in academia and are utilized in many areas, particularly centering around pedagogical growth and learning design.

While cases of CoPs are found more often in other areas of higher education, there are many aspects of academic librarianship in which CoPs prove to be both applicable and useful. For example, the University of Idaho Libraries utilizes CoPs for their newly hired tenure-track librarians by incorporating peer-mentoring, which allows new instruction librarians to create connections within their teaching practice. At Vanderbilt University, public services librarians participated in a CoP to help strengthen their teaching identities (more details about this are discussed shortly). The instruction coordinator at Monroe Library, Loyola University New Orleans, used a CoP to build the pedagogical skills of teaching librarians and foster a culture of learning within the instruction team (Willey, 2014).

Wenger (1998) suggests three dimensions of CoPs that can help guide the organization of the group and the subsequent discussions: *mutual engagement* (engaging in similar activities, which leads to a feeling of community); *joint enterprise* (an accountability and set of processes that are negotiated by the participants); and *shared repertoire* ("a set of shared resources including stories, artifacts, tools, styles, actions, historical events, discourses or concepts produced or adopted during the lifecycle of the CoP" [Kim, 2015, p. 2]). Each of these areas proves beneficial to teaching CoP, especially in academic libraries. Even for those librarians working in robust liaison programs, instruction librarians can often feel isolated, particularly if they are working in remote locations or without access to shared resources. This is particularly challenging when a library either does not have a liaison program, has just one or two teaching librarians, or has a distributed model of teaching that occurs across the library in different departments. A CoP not only provides a sense of community around a shared job function (i.e., instruction) but can also serve as a way to provide additional resources and support to librarians across a variety of departments.

Benefits for Instruction Programs

While CoPs are useful for individual learning and development around a shared interest, they are also extremely useful for building community across library units. Henrich and Attebury (2010) remark that a CoP can "raise awareness of how current ideas, projects, and research related to each [department] serve the larger organization as a whole. This collaboration itself can lead to idea creation, innovation, and project success" (p. 161). This notion of cross-unit collaboration lends itself particularly well to teaching CoP in libraries, where instruction happens in many units. Instruction program Coordinators can build a robust CoP by including academic liaison librarians, Special Collections librarians, librarians working in digital scholarship or scholarly communications, and technical services librarians that provide training and instruction for patrons or colleagues. The perspectives and backgrounds of the librarians teaching in these areas will enrich the conversations and, ideally, encourage colleagues to think about their teaching in new and different ways.

In addition to the professional development and growth opportunities afforded by CoPs, they can also be used as a way of modeling and reinforcing active engagement techniques. Kim (2015) notes that "the CoP approach has potential to support situated learning, given its resemblance to apprenticeship. It is an effective way of learning that helps students internalize the knowledge that they obtain from classroom activities through practice" (p. 49).

Organizing a CoP for instruction librarians can also create a safe place to share challenges or concerns about their teaching. Librarians may feel more comfortable sharing their pedagogical worries or best practices within a small, consistent group of colleagues rather than at a staff meeting or in a larger, more formal gathering. Additionally, CoPs are useful for not only fostering individual learning and development around a shared interest, but for building community across library units. Building these cross-departmental communities is particularly important when discussing teacher identity, in part because it creates a level playing field and common language for librarians that teach or train in multiple areas (e.g., subject liaisons, electronic resources librarians, and functional specialists such as digital scholarship librarians).

Getting Started with a CoP

Pyrko, Dörfler, and Eden (2017) recommend reflecting on the following questions when deciding whether or not to implement a Community of Practice: "Does it make sense to look at [a] social structure as a CoP? Would it be worthwhile or rather counterproductive?" (p. 405). They further note that "cultivating CoPs is not about deciding to 'set up a CoP', but about making conscious efforts to learn more about one's own learning and ways of improving it" (Pyrko, Dörfler, & Eden, 2017, p. 405). The following strategies will also provide guidance to Instruction Coordinators as they begin to plan and organize a CoP.

Articulate the Context

Wenger (2002) recommends starting a CoP by setting the context, which should clearly align with strategic goals (notably of the instruction program, but should also be tied to the library's or institution's strategic teaching and learning goals). This context, along with the goals and intended outcome(s) for the CoP should be clearly communicated to all participants and can be used as a sort of "interest statement," which may help in gathering participants.

Librarians at Vanderbilt University participated in a CoP focusing on developing teacher identity, using the ACRL *Roles and Strengths of Teaching Librarians* (Amsberry et al., 2017) as a guiding document. The following learning goals were shared with librarians during the recruitment phase:

- Recognize different types of roles discussed in the ACRL document;
- Identify your own role as a teaching librarian;
- Evaluate how your role is complementary with others; and
- Leverage, through instruction, the strengths of each six roles (Mallon & Smiley, 2019).

Articulating these goals provided context and helped set expectations for what librarians could expect, which is crucial when pulling in librarians that do not have a background in teaching or may not be familiar with the concept of a CoP. Essentially, the Instruction Coordinator should be prepared to fully articulate what librarians can expect to get out of their participation in the CoP. The answers may vary by individual, but there should be a clear connection to department goals.

Center the Conversations

Similar to Wenger's (1998) three dimensions, developing shared talking points can help provide a framework and context for a teaching CoP. Organizing the CoP meetings around a shared document or particular area of discussion helps keep the meetings moving and gives participants something to focus on. Pyrko, Dörfler, and Eden (2017) suggest identifying "specific key problems and hot topics" that are relevant to all members of the organization, trying to focus on things that members feel particularly passionate about. Discussion topics can be around anything related to teaching and learning, including individual teaching/pedagogy styles; active learning techniques; the ACRL *Framework*; or student learning assessment. Discussing shared documents, such as the ACRL *Roles and Strengths* document, as mentioned previously, can also provide readily available talking points; in the Vanderbilt example, participants read each "role" before the meeting and came prepared to discuss how it related to their own identity as a teaching librarian (Mallon & Smiley, 2019). For teaching CoPs, using documents like the ACRL *Roles and Strengths* or the ACRL *Framework* can also connect back to discussions related to teacher identity, the purpose of an instruction or teaching and learning program, and issues related to student learning.

Keep Members Engaged

It can be hard to keep momentum and participation in CoPs going beyond the initial start-up; however, Instruction Coordinators must encourage the teaching librarians they work with to participate in activities that foster development and community. To keep librarians and staff engaged, the Coordinator should consider a timeline that will allow for regular participation that complements day-to-day activities. This is particularly important when involving teaching librarians, who do not often have time for supplementary activities during their busy teaching times. Mallon and Smiley (2019) note that shorter time frames for CoPs creates more engagement and sustained interest; they found that a CoP spread over an entire academic year resulted in low participation by the end of the year.

On the other hand, creating too much structure can also prove challenging; Pyrko, Dörfler, and Eden (2017) found that one of the biggest problems with non-successful CoPs is "neglecting the organic nature of the development" (p. 402). A sustainable CoP provides an overall structure but allows for flexibility and evolution in the discussions (again, keep in mind the inherent goodness of "messy" problems and questions) (Bass, 1999; Bass & Eynon, 1998).

Grow Beyond the Library

A final strategy for increasing participation and impact is for Instruction Coordinators to facilitate and sustain a culture of teaching and learning in a larger context, perhaps through CoP participation beyond the library. CoPs can develop through many different channels, and likely, the more diverse the participation in the CoP, the more growth will occur. As previously discussed, a CoP could be comprised of library staff from across all departments within the library, but it could be made up of institutional colleagues focusing on shared topics such as student learning assessment, open educational resources (OER), or lifelong learning. Alexander and Bradley (2010) advocate for reaching out to those colleagues across campus for whom improving teaching and learning are also core values; this has the twin benefits of providing librarians with an opportunity to find kindred spirits on campus and share their own instructional expertise. Librarians should also be encouraged to seek out communities to engage with outside their universities; cross-institutional CoPs provide new perspectives on similar problems and have the added benefit of sustaining growth even if the participants move to new institutions (Cater-Steel, McDonald, Albion, & Redmond, 2017).

PEER TEACHING OBSERVATIONS

Finally, another strategy for encouraging reflection and building community related to teaching and learning is through peer observation of teaching. Bandy (2017) cites several benefits for incorporating peer review of teaching, including encouraging experimentation in the classroom, less reliance on student evaluations, and also, germaine to this chapter's previous discussions, enabling "teaching to be a community endeavor" (para 4).

Alabi and Weare (2013) note two different types of peer observation programs: an informal observation process, which is considered formative and is primarily used for improving teaching; and a summative evaluation process that is used to evaluate the quality of teaching and is commonly found in the tenure and promotion process (p. 7). This more formalized instruction observation requirement, which is often viewed as a mandate from the top down, has the potential to cause undue stress, particularly for librarians that are not comfortable with their teaching identity. There is little the Coordinator can do if the observation is indeed a requirement for advancement; however, the Instruction Coordinator might create a supplementary observation program that is made up of instructional colleagues (i.e., peers), and not supervisors or tenure committee members. This could help teaching librarians view the peer observation as a way to learn and grow with their colleagues.

While the teaching observation program does not have to be too intense or formal, it should still include some level of rigor to ensure that the process is beneficial for the participants. The observational relationship should be open and transparent and grounded in an environment of trust: "Peer reviews also function best when reviewers have commitments to integrity, fair-mindedness, privacy, and understanding the reasoning behind the teaching choices of the person under review" (Bandy, 2017, para. 11). A peer teaching observation program has great potential to enhance the teaching and learning culture within the library.

CONTINUING THE PARADIGM SHIFT

Teaching culture, as with any framework or paradigm for shared communication and values, will likely shift as the culture of the library or institution changes:

> the idea of culture, the definition of culture, and the forms of culture within an institution change as the needs of higher education changes. Whether or not a particular culture is considered fundamental to the success of an institution, it is valuable to understand its depth and nature. Institutional culture may provide insight into the motivations of individuals, strengthen plans for development, and act as a powerful catalyst for change. (Kustra et al., 2014, p. 7)

Additionally, Roxå, Mårtensson, and Alveteg (2011) provide a much-needed reminder that cultural change is not immediate: "actions driving change in one direction will most likely be counteracted by balancing forces from within the culture; and the result of a specific action may not show itself until after some time of delay" (p. 105).

Readers may be thinking to themselves, "but . . . our culture hasn't budged for years!" If that is the case, never fear; while fostering and maintaining a culture of teaching and learning can be challenging and most certainly takes time, even small steps go a long way to creating a dialogue around teaching and learning that will positively impact the librarians involved in teaching, as well as the instruction program as a whole. Just as the previous chapter stressed the criticality of taking stock of where an instruction program "sits," as additional aspects of program development are explored in future chapters, it will be equally important to have a sense of the current culture related to teaching and learning—both in the library and on campus.

Chapter Four

To Frame or Not to Frame?

A BACKGROUND ON INFORMATION LITERACY GUIDING DOCUMENTS

When it was first introduced in 2015, the ACRL's *Framework for Information Literacy for Higher Education* (ACRL, 2015) (ACRL *Framework*) created many opportunities for librarians to reconsider their pedagogical practices and invigorate their information literacy instruction. Along with the excitement came a certain amount of stress and trepidation from some libraries that had built their instruction programs around the *Information Literacy Competency Standards for Higher Education* (originally approved in January 2000) (ACRL *Standards*). Nevertheless, when the ACRL *Framework* was adopted by the ACRL Board in 2016, librarians were presented with the opportunity to discuss information literacy in new ways, including offering new pathways for broaching information literacy with faculty. In the years since the ACRL *Framework* was adopted, many Instruction Coordinators have had to have serious conversations with their teaching librarians about revisions to instruction program goals and outcomes, revised curriculum maps, new methods of integrating into general education programs, and more. As mentioned, this has been challenging, particularly for small libraries and instruction teams who suffer from both limited time and resources, as well as for larger instruction programs, which may have developed an extensive ACRL *Standards*-based suite of lesson plans, curriculum maps, and more.

Also worth noting is that the ACRL *Framework*, while officially adopted by ACRL in the United States, is not the only method by which instruction programs can structure their work. Other information literacy models, such as the *Alexandria Proclamation on Information Literacy* (International Federation of Library Associations and Institutions, 2005), the Society of College, National, and University Libraries *7 Pillars of Information Literacy* (SCONUL, 2011), and the *Australian and New Zealand Information Literacy Framework* (Bundy, 2004), are also excellent guiding documents that provide a helpful roadmap for structuring an information literacy program. For further exploration, Grassian (2017) provides a helpfully comprehensive and robust list of information literacy guiding documents for a variety of institution types and education levels.

There does exist a fairly extensive body of literature on the ACRL *Framework* and its predecessors, as they are the primary structures by which the academic library profession in the United States discusses information literacy work. Because of that, this chapter presents an overview of the ACRL *Framework* and how it can be used in instruction program organization and development; this chapter also presents (with perhaps a bit more depth) several alternatives for exploring the underpinnings of an instruction program. Furthermore, this chapter is not meant to pit the ACRL *Framework* against any other, nor does it claim that any one document or guidelines are supreme above all others. Likewise, it is important to point out that no one document, including the ACRL *Framework*, is a perfect-match, one-size-fits-all solution to academic information literacy programs. Rather, this chapter presents strategies for engaging with the ACRL *Framework* as well as alternatives for approaching information literacy instruction in a way that meets the needs of the campus/program/library, and, perhaps most importantly, the students!

INCORPORATING THE ACRL *FRAMEWORK FOR INFORMATION LITERACY*

A healthy amount of literature (Farkas, 2017; Foasburg, 2015; Hess, 2015; among others), open educational resources (e.g., the Information Literacy Sandbox, http://sandbox.acrl.org/, and Project Cora, https://www.projectcora.org/), and standards-to-framework maps (Hovious, 2015; "Information Literacy Plan," 2018) have been published that advocate for using the ACRL *Framework* to plan individual information literacy sessions and assessment of student learning. These resources are extremely useful and have helped many librarians in adjusting their teaching to incorporate the six frames. However, this section discusses using the ACRL *Framework* as a foundation for an entire instruction program. As a Coordinator, how might one structure their program in an ACRL *Framework*–influenced way? This can take shape in several different configurations. For instance, the ACRL *Framework* can be used to guide the development of an instruction program's mission and learning goals. Falcone and McCartin (2018) list several tips for libraries looking to use the ACRL *Framework* for the development of student learning outcomes (SLOs):

- *Set aside time for reflection and editing.* Rather than immersing your team in this process throughout one or two meetings, space the conversations so there is adequate time to reflect on the drafts. Having an online editable document so people can edit the outcomes when inspired and able is helpful.
- *As the facilitator, continue to motivate and encourage individuals, especially when they contribute to the working document.* If you notice an individual has been inactive, reach out and encourage their ideas.
- *Remember that this is a group effort.* Facilitators must be careful not to dominate conversations and should not take sole responsibility for writing the SLOs.
- *Remember that you do not have to incorporate every aspect of the Framework into your SLOs.* Some parts of the Framework may be out of the scope for your instruction program and may be more appropriately integrated in other teaching activities, settings, sessions, or library courses. (para. 19)

Jacobson and Gibson (2015) recommend that to "develop a larger program architecture using the ACRL *Framework*, information literacy librarians will need to conduct systematic curriculum analyses and design curriculum maps to identify those courses and programs that are the most natural 'fit' or homes for the six Frames" (p. 104). This analysis is already a recommended part of program development (see Chapter 2), but if a library's teaching and learning program is going to develop its goals and vision from the ACRL *Framework*, then a restructuring may be in order.

Similarly, the ACRL *Framework* also provides an excellent model for assessing student learning at the program level; Gammons and Inge (2017) used the *Framework* as an impetus to move student learning assessment practices away from "passive" and distant methods to a method "that combines the scalability of a survey with the intentionality of qualitative research" (p. 170). Gammons and Inge's (2017) assessment strategy (having students tweet their "ah-ha" moment) was piloted in 12 sections of a first-year composition program, and while this may not necessarily be scalable for an entire instruction program, it does provide some insight into the more innovative and flexible ways the ACRL *Framework* is guiding assessment of information literacy skills.

Aside from student learning and assessment, Instruction Coordinators may also wish to use the ACRL *Framework* as a model for developing librarians as teachers (more about teacher development, from a non-ACRL *Framework* perspective, can be found next, as well as in Chapter 3). Hess

(2015) advocates for viewing the ACRL *Framework* through the lens of adult learning theories (e.g., Transformative Learning Theory; Social Learning Theory) as a way of fostering community and collaboration among instruction librarians and as a way for instruction program leaders to motivate librarians to adapt to new ways of approaching teaching and learning.

A WORD ON THRESHOLD CONCEPTS

When evaluating models for program development, it can also be useful to examine some of the methods by which students learn the skills and behaviors that will help them succeed as academics, particularly in their chosen field of study. Threshold concepts, which can be thought of as "portals" to new ways of thinking and learning, provide one such way of viewing learning in an academic and disciplinary-focused context (Meyer, 2008; Meyer & Land, 2003). Barradell and Kennedy-Jones (2015) note that:

> Threshold concepts are a pivotal idea; firstly, because they seem to establish the means for academics with little curricula expertise to engage more confidently with teaching and learning discussions, and secondly, because they form the basis of a conceptual framework that has the capacity to draw together many important related curriculum, teaching and learning elements. (p. 538)

In the context of this chapter, threshold concepts are also connected closely with the ACRL *Framework*. The study of threshold concepts and information literacy, as developed by Hofer, Townsend, and Brunetti (2012), "involves going further by asking what transformative, integrative concept must be grasped in order for students to move forward from that point" (p. 393). These threshold concepts can provide the foundation for the overall instruction program structure, allowing librarians to "devise targeted curricula by prioritizing trouble spots in a way that professional standards documents do not" (Hofer, Townsend, & Brunetti, 2012, p. 403). Hofer, Townsend, and Brunetti (2013) further elaborated on this approach as the ACRL task force began their revisions to the ACRL *Standards* document by suggesting that, within the realm of information literacy *as a discipline*, threshold concepts can "[clarify] our focus and [limit] our content to that which is unique to our discipline" (p. 111).

The incorporation and reliance on threshold concepts in the ACRL *Framework* (as well as the positioning of information literacy as a discipline) has indeed ignited multiple arguments amongst library professionals. On one side is the argument against the ACRL *Framework*, in that it ignores the disciplinary threshold concepts students must achieve to show mastery in their academic field (see Beilin [2015] and Wilkinson [2014] for early critiques), while others argue in favor of the ACRL *Framework*, because it positions the six frames as a flexible opportunity for teaching students transferable, lifelong learning skills (Fister, 2014; Gibson & Jacobson, 2014). Fister (2014) argues that librarians are, for the most part, unable to "agree as a profession on which troublesome concepts are most transformative and essential or exactly how librarians should rethink their instructional efforts to nudge students across those thresholds" (para. 5). Information literacy aside, because threshold concepts, in particular, are situated squarely within the disciplines, they can also provide an opening for examining an instruction program's structure outside of the traditional means. For example, the program could be structured in a scaffolded approach, with "big picture" interdisciplinary transferable research skills, which build the foundation for specific disciplinary threshold concepts.

Again, the purpose of this chapter is not to encourage or implore Instruction Coordinators to structure their programs wholly around the ACRL *Framework*, but rather to provide several options. As mentioned earlier, what works for one program will not work for another, and it is unfair to expect all academic library instruction programs to embrace the ACRL *Framework* without examining other alternatives that may work better for their institutional size or context.

ALTERNATIVES TO THE ACRL *FRAMEWORK*

Despite the many benefits of using the ACRL *Framework* as a model, there are also many reasons librarians may choose not to utilize the ACRL *Framework* as the guiding document for their instruction program. These reasons are myriad, from staffing issues to the time it takes to transfer curriculum maps or learning outcomes from the previous version of the ACRL *Standards* to a critique of the use of threshold concepts (Wilkinson, 2014) to a lack of support outside of the library (or even inside the library). Grassian (2017) encourages librarians to remember that "many alternative IL/MIL [information literacy/media & information literacy] models, conceptual approaches, frameworks, and standards have been developed for different educational and age levels" (p. 233).

One argument against building an instruction program entirely around the ACRL *Framework* is that it is a document produced and adopted by the academic librarian profession and thus can be seen as insular and nonrelevant beyond the library walls. Are faculty aware that it exists? Should they be? Setting aside the argument for advocacy and education regarding the ACRL *Framework*, it may be necessary for instruction program Coordinators to explore other models that are more aligned to their program or university goals.

Outcomes Alignment

One option that is arguably less structured, but perhaps has a lower barrier to entry is for librarians to let institutional needs drive the formation of the instruction program and its content. This can be easier to accomplish than specifically using the ACRL *Framework* as the impetus for program outcomes (as discussed earlier), since many programs and departments often have learning outcomes clearly stated on their websites, or accessible simply by contacting the program's education coordinators or department chairs. Some disciplinary accrediting bodies (such as the Accreditation Council for Business Schools and Programs [ACBSP] or the Council for the Accreditation of Educator Professionals [CAEP]) also have specific learning outcomes related to information literacy, disciplinary research skills, or critical thinking. Mapping information literacy skills to existing accreditation and departmental learning outcomes is a crucial step in not only getting buy-in from faculty but also to make a positive and authentic impact on student learning. While Chapters 2 and 6 delve into more detail on the importance and benefits of using curriculum mapping to align the instruction program with institutional priorities, it is worth mentioning again here that an instruction program is most successful when it is distinctly tied to these priorities, rather than operating as a stand-alone entity. Jankowski and Marshall (2017) stress the need to think in the bigger picture, aligning outcomes at a higher level than just individual courses:

> Pathways focused on learning, as opposed to syllabi or articulation agreements of specific courses, have the greatest opportunity to be beneficial when they are utilized as a means to reach shared consensus, scaffold learning opportunities, and make connections across systems based on students and their learning [. . .] in the dizzying array of learning opportunities available to students, clear communication becomes essential if students are to understand why we ask them to move through our curricular learning experiences as we do. (p. 41)

Aligning information literacy outcomes directly to the curriculum is a critical and necessary process, but it can feel somewhat disconnected and formalized—particularly if this work is done solely by the Instruction Coordinator. This can result in teaching librarians that do not have buy-in to the program's direction and may cause some anxiety or frustration in librarians that feel as though they are being force-fed learning outcomes without any say in how it affects their teaching. To avoid this, Coordinators can engage their team in shared development of the program's learning outcomes (this is similar to the shared development of an instruction program statement, which is discussed in more detail in the next chapter), creating cohesion and communication in what can feel like an isolated activity. An added benefit of this approach allows for further alignment of the instruction team, which can be particularly useful for community development and a team-teaching approach. Again, the program learning outcomes can and should be tied to campus/department/program outcomes, and they can reflect some of the conceptual ideas that make up the ACRL *Framework*, but they can also be a way of communicating the instruction programs' shared values and beliefs when it comes to information literacy and other types of skill development.

Signature Pedagogies

Librarians in teaching and learning programs are continually looking for ways to integrate information literacy skill development into students' curricular and co-curricular work. At the same time, faculty are also exploring ways of addressing the need for specific skill development in different academic fields:

> educating students to practice the intellectual moves and values of experts in the field has been a subtext of most disciplinary learning outcomes. Some faculty and departments are explicit about teaching their students to think more like disciplinary experts, whereas others focus on disciplinary content and related skills, with expert thinking an implicit goal. (Haynie, Chick, & Gurung, 2009, p. 3)

Librarians are uniquely positioned to fill the role of fitting within and alongside this paradigm, both teaching students how to research like an expert *and* guiding students in the development of transferable skills that guide their thinking and information-seeking behavior.

Shulman (2005) defines signature pedagogies as a fundamental characteristic form of teaching and learning that focuses on the fundamental knowledge practices one must be aware of in a given professional field. Shulman (2005) further states that signature pedagogies:

> implicitly define what counts as knowledge in a field and how things become known. They define how knowledge is analyzed, criticized, accepted, or discarded. They define the functions of expertise in a field, the locus of authority, and the privileges of rank and standing [. . .] these pedagogies even determine the architectural design of educational institutions, which in turn serves to perpetuate these approaches. (p. 54)

Utilizing signature pedagogies to situate information literacy within disciplinary curricula serves several purposes: it presents these skills and concepts within the language of the discipline, which is particularly useful for facilitating communication with both faculty and advanced students (upper-level undergraduates as well as graduate and professional students); it allows librarians to advocate the value of teaching general research skills in conjunction with field-specific skill development; and, it provides a pathway for students to make research connections both inside and outside of their courses.

Haynie, Chick, and Gurung (2009) note that "as students gradually and metacognitively recognize the different yet overlapping ways of thinking, knowing, and doing within their different courses, they begin to see a conversation among their courses, allowing them to situate themselves within that conversation and shift from one perspective to another" (p. 12). The Instruction Coordinator is certainly positioned to make the argument that the library's teaching and learning program both complements and adds to this conversation. As with threshold concepts (discussed in more detail previously), signature pedagogies can be "used as a diagnostic for teaching and learning approaches, highlight areas in need of adjustment and refinement, and point to avenues for potential change to specific course design as well as larger curricula development" (Lüdert, n.d., para. 7).

Librarians as Teachers and Researchers

There are other philosophies and schema that can provide the structure within which an instruction program is developed. For example, a library might ground its instruction program not in a guiding set of standards or document produced by a professional association, but rather by investing in its librarians as teachers or educators first. These professional development models are explored more in Chapter 3, but are also discussed in this chapter as a way to structure an instruction program. Investing in the pedagogical skills of librarians can go a long way in providing relevance and promoting the value of librarians as partners in teaching and learning. Carroll and Klipfel (2019) provide a stark outlook that speaks to the dangers of not systematically developing a librarian's teaching skills and comfort:

> for a passionate disciplinary faculty member who values their students' time, the experience of working with an overwhelmed, ineffective library instructor can create lasting negative impressions, even among disciplinary faculty inclined to be open to meaningful instructional partnerships with library faculty. (p. 113)

Providing more grounding in a librarians' disciplinary and pedagogical expertise is certainly a looser way of structuring an instruction program, but teaching librarians (particularly those working in a disciplinary-liaison model) may find the flexibility to approach their teaching from an individualized, research-based focus more rewarding and successful. The Scholarship of Teaching and Learning (SoTL) lends itself well to structuring an instruction program by positioning information literacy concepts within the disciplinary context of the course, as well as by aligning the librarian as a teacher-researcher. SoTL is rooted in pedagogical inquiry, thus positioning librarians participating in an instruction program to approach their work from a paradigm that encourages data collection, observation, and making thoughtful changes to one's teaching practice (McNiff & Hays, 2017).

Threshold concepts, introduced earlier in this chapter, can also provide a strong foundation for positioning librarians as teachers and researchers. In addition to using threshold concepts as a way of determining the curricular focus of an instruction program, Barradell and Kennedy-Jones (2015) also suggest that they can aid in pedagogical development:

> The opportunity for educators to engage with others (including students in their discipline) and to identify troublesome ideas is valuable. The activity of deconstructing a subject or discipline, thinking about the best way to teach and learn it, reflects the instructive and useful potential of the threshold concept framework. (p. 538)

Examining threshold concepts, either from an information literacy perspective or from within liaison librarians' subject areas, can provide robust opportunities for teaching and learning research projects. If all librarians within a teaching program participate in SoTL research and practice, they can make holistic and more systematic changes to the teaching and learning program based on a drive to improve the student learning experience.

INFORMATION LITERACY BY ANY OTHER NAME

Regardless of the model by which an instruction program is organized, it is crucial for Coordinators, and for the teaching librarians working within the program, to remember the program's purpose and goals. For many libraries, this purpose is to enhance and improve student learning. Instruction Coordinators should keep the underlying goal(s) in mind when making decisions on how to structure a learning environment, and continuously engage their instruction librarian colleagues in the exploration of both how their teaching aligns with the program goals and how it enhances student learning. To facilitate connections and conversations with faculty, it is also important to consider language. Do faculty know what "information literacy" means? Do they need to know? Successful Instruction Coordinators often have varied ways of talking about information literacy integration, whether they are relying on the ACRL *Framework*, institutional or departmental learning outcomes, or disciplinary threshold concepts. These terms are often used interchangeably by librarians, too (and are used often in this book!): critical thinking, disciplinary research skills, lifelong learning, digital and media literacy, and so on. This approach also raises the option of aligning the ACRL *Framework* concepts (i.e., the six frames) without necessarily referencing ACRL's publication (Guth, Arnold, Bielat, Perez-Stable, & Vander

Meer, 2018); thus, program development does not have to fall strictly within the guidelines of the ACRL *Framework* document itself. Grassian (2017) recommends the following questions as guideposts for framing an information literacy program:

- What does "library instruction" mean to you and your community, however you label it?
- What do members of your community already know about information researching?
- What do you expect the learners in your community to know and be able to do on their own related to information researching, and at which age and educational levels? (p. 233)

Likewise, Jacobson and Gibson (2015) note that:

> it is less important that the strict terminology of the *Framework* be used in discussions with faculty about assignment and course design than that these core principles be honored: (1) extended student engagement with the big ideas of the Framework, (2) students' critical self-reflection on their learning of those ideas, and (3) student creativity in participating in the information ecosystem—whether through a blog, a multimedia project, a digital storytelling session, or participation in a student panel on a topic important on campus. (p.105)

Recognizing the language used on one's campus to discuss student learning and skill development and hitting on what resonates with faculty will go a long way in ensuring the success of an instruction program.

The next chapter provides more detail on writing an instruction program statement, which is an important step for articulating the library's vision on student learning both within the library organization and across campus. Having a well written, clear, and relatable instruction program statement will set the foundation for successfully communicating the library's role in teaching and learning.

Chapter Five

Writing an Instruction Program Statement

LIGHTING THE WAY, STAKING A CLAIM: USES AND BENEFITS OF AN INSTRUCTION PROGRAM STATEMENT

In the same way that no two instruction programs are alike, or that no two Instruction Coordinators are alike, an instruction program statement reflects the specific context, resources, and philosophy of its library and its institution. Although these statements tend to have some elements in common, each instruction program statement is as unique as a fingerprint.

An instruction program statement can be seen as a mission statement, a vision statement, or a statement of purpose for the program, for those who teach in it and for those who participate in it as learners or stakeholders. As Benjes-Small and Miller (2017) note:

> In order for an instruction program to succeed, the program and its goals need to be understood and valued by other leaders in your library, disciplinary faculty, and other leaders and administrators throughout your institution. [. . .] Before reaching out beyond the library, though, coordinators need to ensure that others within the library understand the purpose, scope, and value of the instruction program. (p. 149)

ACRL's *Guidelines* (2011) recommend that an academic library "should have a written mission statement for its instructional program." Putting this statement in writing helps to disseminate the "scope, purpose, and value" highlighted by Benjes-Small and Miller (2017), and allows the library, and the Instruction Coordinator, to carefully craft a message about the library's role in teaching and learning, rather than leaving this role open to ambiguity and varied interpretation.

A program statement is a foundational document that addresses several audiences, both inside and outside the library. It speaks to the instructional team by laying out a vision for how each instructor and each instruction session relate to the program as a whole. It helps others within the library understand the teaching role of their instruction colleagues and expresses the value of this work to the overall library mission. To constituents outside the library, the program statement sets expectations for students, faculty, and administrators, while articulating the library's role in teaching and learning on campus. Ideally, an instruction program statement is not an isolated, one-off document, but rather is embedded within, or in conversation with, other statements from the library and the institution about the overall mission, vision, and goals, as well as perspectives on teaching, learning, and research. Above all, it "should not be viewed as a pro forma, static and uninspiring fragment of verbiage, but rather as a dynamic document" (Noe, 2013, p. 16).

An instruction program statement is immensely valuable for the Instruction Coordinator. The process of creating the statement, much like the process of taking stock of an instruction program and the teaching and learning landscape of the institution (see Chapter 2), is an opportunity to consider the tacit beliefs and current understanding of an existing instruction program. By using a participatory process to arrive at a program statement, discussed later in this chapter, the Instruction Coordinator and their team will surface ideas, some of which may have persisted despite no longer reflecting reality. Discussion, debate, and consensus are a part of the process. The program statement both reflects and helps to set program priorities; it provides a framework for program assessment (see Chapter 7) and can be used to guide goal-setting for individual teaching librarians or for the entire team of instructors. It offers a reminder that each session, tutorial, or learning object is part of the library's bigger teaching and learning program, and it may emphasize how library instruction complements other teaching and learning on campus or feeds into the institution's mission. A program statement can be used to promote and raise the visibility of library instruction, and to assist the Instruction Coordinator in their advocacy for the program (see Chapter 6). Finally, the program statement "stakes a claim" on teaching and learning for the library by elucidating that the instruction program is one of the library's contributions to its home institution.

For this chapter, it is useful to differentiate between a *program statement* and a *program plan*. A program statement expresses the vision, purpose, and underlying principles of the library's teaching and learning activity. It is a high-level view of what students, faculty, administrators, and collaborators can expect from library instruction. It is not the specific learning outcomes of an individual session, but an indication of who teaches and what they teach, in what contexts or modes, and to which intended audiences of learners. A program plan, on the other hand, may detail the precise terrain of teaching and learning within the library; a plan calls out particular components of the program, including sequenced instruction within a discipline or scaffolded workshops on research skills. The statement (vision and overview) and the plan (specific instructional activities) should complement and reinforce each other.

ELEMENTS OF AN INSTRUCTION PROGRAM STATEMENT

Drafting an instruction program statement is the point at which the environmental scan outlined in Chapter 2, the reflection on building a culture of instruction in Chapter 3, and the consideration of information literacy and the ACRL *Framework* in Chapter 4 come together. The ACRL *Guidelines* (2011) offer guidance for articulating the purpose of a library instruction program; they state that this written statement should:

- situate the program in the context of its institution's mission and needs;
- involve campus stakeholders in the creation of goals and outcomes;
- define information literacy and align with the ACRL *Framework*;
- emphasize the diversity of learners within the institution;
- champion library instruction's uses beyond the classroom, for example, for careers and lifelong learning; and
- undergo regular review and revision as needed.

The exhortation to define information literacy and align with the ACRL *Framework* is a matter best considered in the context of an institution (see Chapter 4). This is also where the environmental scanning work recommended in Chapters 2 and 4 will come in handy.

The format or template of the instruction program statement will likely look different for each library, but Coordinators should consult similar statements in their library or institution and attempt to mirror the format. In a survey of UK academic library instruction programs, Corrall (2007) found that:

> [instruction program] mission statements varied in format, content and length. A common form was a headline statement of a few lines, followed by bullet points, with information literacy featuring in one point, though often alongside other items and sometimes towards the end of a long list. Another type of statement used complete sentences, rather than bullets, typically 110–120 words long. The wording also varied: several mentioned "training," some "developing" or "teaching" and one "coaching" in "information skills," "information handling skills" or "transferable information skills." Others shifted the

focus from provider to client, e.g., "enabling" or "helping" students (and sometimes staff) to acquire or develop skills. (para. 32)

When considering the language of the program statement, Coordinators should take care to avoid jargon and ensure consistency and alignment with the language and tone of other library or institutional mission statements. Noe (2013) addresses the instinct to fall back on more traditional conventions for describing library instruction efforts, noting:

> while it may be a comfortable habit to call our program by an old, familiar name, it is time to stop using "user education" and "bibliographic instruction." Such terms may be shorthand for those deeply rooted in the profession, but they confuse those who are not as well versed in the professional jargon of an MLS degree program, and they directly impact effectiveness and success. As professionals, we must strive to be more diligent, deliberate and consistent with language and word choices. (p. 12)

A related point of consideration is whether or not to make the program statement public, such as publishing on the library's instruction program website or via an annual report. On the one hand, if the program statement is being used for internal evaluation of teaching librarians or is being used to guide program planning and development, it may likely need to stay internal to the library. However, a clear and concise message about the purpose of the library's instruction program, particularly when it is situated within the context of the greater teaching and learning environment on campus, is a great tool for communication. Similarly, a program statement that aligns with curricular goals and institutional or programmatic learning outcomes can assist in the Coordinator's advocacy work (see Chapter 6). Wells and Young (1994) assert that the program statement is crucial for communicating the functionality of a program or library; it also "lend[s] constancy to the planning process and serve[s] as an authority to which persons involved in the project can refer" (p. 146). Instruction program statements are not one-size-fits-all, and while one can use the ACRL *Guidelines* (and others) to draft their statement, the format should take a second place to content.

Articulating the Big Picture View of Teaching and Learning

An important aspect of the statement content that the Instruction Coordinator should consider is the big picture: the vision for teaching and learning that guides the educational efforts at the library-system and institutional levels. This goes back to the elements discussed in Chapters 3 and 4, and requires the Coordinator to use the environmental scan to help create a picture of the culture for teaching and learning in the library and on campus. Once this is determined, the Coordinator can then more clearly articulate how the instruction program fits into that bigger picture. When drafting the instruction program statement, the Coordinator should not only reference, but also attempt to incorporate, elements of relevant campus programs and strategic initiatives into their teaching and learning program mission (Noe, 2013). One method for articulating the instruction program's importance to the overall teaching and learning mission of the university is to describe how library partnerships extend beyond the library instruction classroom, such as through service learning opportunities or co-curricular outreach activities. Additionally, the Coordinator can highlight the ideals and higher-level goals of the program (this is discussed in more detail in the following section on diversity and inclusion).

AN INCLUSIVE PROCESS FOR DRAFTING A PROGRAM STATEMENT

Once the essential elements of the plan have been identified, it is time to start drafting the statement itself. Farkas, quoted by Benjes-Small and Miller (2017), notes that "[being] a leader does not mean being the sole person to come up with a vision for the future. [The Coordinator's] role is to facilitate the development of a *shared* vision for the future of [the] instruction program" (p. 157). When drafting the program statement, the Instruction Coordinator has a unique opportunity to create an inclusive process by leveraging the expertise and experience of their teaching librarian colleagues.

Librarian Teaching Statements

One way this can be accomplished is by incorporating the teaching statements of individual librarians that work under the context of the instruction program. A teaching statement:

> is a purposeful and reflective essay about the author's teaching beliefs and practices. It is an individual narrative that includes not only one's beliefs about the teaching and learning process, but also concrete examples of the ways in which he or she enacts these beliefs in the classroom. (Center for Teaching, 2019, para. 1).

These statements should connect the work of teaching librarians with that of the instruction program, and show a clear alignment to the program's strategic vision and goals. If librarians have existing teaching statements, the Instruction Coordinator can work with their colleagues to review the statements for salient points that should be included in the overall program statement. This is a good moment to look for alignment (or lack thereof) with individuals' teaching statements or philosophies with that of identified program goals.

If the librarians have not yet articulated their teaching statements, then the Coordinator can engage the team in an exercise to determine how the program statement can be drafted to collectively meet the library's teaching and learning mission. Blakesley and Baron (2002) describe the process of developing an instruction program mission statement and goals as a follow-up to attending ACRL immersion:

> All instruction librarians were involved in the process of approving a mission statement to guide the instruction program in the future. We also agreed upon programmatic goals to guide our instruction activities. This was significant for our staff, who had heretofore thought of instruction as an extension of reference—a means of getting students to the correct books or databases. Thinking about the program in terms of information literacy training and skill development helped us redefine what we do. (p. 152)

Benjes-Small and Miller (2017) also touch on the inclusion of librarians in the process of writing the program statement as a way to build team camaraderie and cohesion, encouraging Coordinators to "think about the role that the instruction program plays within your library, and the role that each person on the team plays within that program" (p. 154).

Incorporating Stakeholder Feedback

The importance of including the feedback of internal (to the library) and external (on campus) stakeholders to guide instruction program development has been touched on many times already. This strategy is equally useful for drafting the program statement, as recommended by the ACRL *Guidelines* (2011). While different constituents (even students) will have varying degrees of investment or interest, engaging them in the process is an important way to increase buy-in to the program itself. Regardless of how involved stakeholders are in the process, it is important to remember that a program statement is also a communication tool:

> By placing your users' needs at the heart of your program and communicating your instructional intent to them through your goals and objectives, you are creating an instruction program that demonstrates your care and concern. Your students become partners in the development process. [. . .] By word and deed you exhibit your respect for your students and their abilities. (Grassian & Kaplowitz, 2001, pp. 146–147)

CREATING SPACE FOR DIVERSITY IN AN INSTRUCTION PROGRAM STATEMENT

As a written encapsulation of an instruction program's core, a program statement provides an excellent opportunity to articulate the library's respect for and commitment to diversity and inclusion. Incorporating elements of inclusive teaching into the instruction program's mission and goals can also aid in strategic alignment. Many universities have stated commitments to inclusion, diversity, equity, and accessibility (IDEA), and incorporating these elements into the planning process and the language of the program statement shows a deeper level of support for this work.

Universal Design for Learning

Universal design for learning (UDL) is a framework that is applied to teaching and learning to create an equitable learning environment, regardless of learning preferences or constraints. Scott, Mcguire, and Shaw (2003) recommend UDL as a proactive practice for designing instruction with the learner in mind. Essentially, the UDL framework means that all learning materials and content should be presented in a way that makes them accessible by all learners; for example, rather than making separate accommodations in a course management system for students with visual impairments, *all* materials in that course should be easy to access and use, no matter what types of learners are in the course. The principles of UDL are based on the overarching goals of providing multiple means of representation ("the 'what' of learning"), providing multiple means of expression ("the 'how' of learning"), and providing multiple means of engagement ("the 'why' of learning") (Chodock & Dolinger, 2009, p. 26).

Articulating a commitment to the accessibility of instructional materials is an important message for an instruction program statement to send and can help guide librarians in the creation of research guides and other learning objects, such as online tutorials (Webb & Hoover, 2015). UDL "holds great potential for expanding inclusive teaching practices in higher education" (Scott, Mcguire, & Shaw, 2003) and incorporating the principles can ensure a more inclusive and welcoming instruction program statement.

Social Justice and Critical Pedagogy

One of the defining features of IDEA work in 21st-century higher education is a focus on social justice and inclusion of marginalized populations. There are some aspects of this in the ACRL *Framework*, notably the frames related to authority, context, and access to information. Social justice work, in particular, "seeks to ensure that all people participate in and benefit equally from a system" (Mathuews, 2016, p. 10), sharing a similar philosophical foundation with UDL. Mathuews (2016) notes that intentionality is also key when increasing diversity and inclusion efforts, particularly for libraries pushing these efforts outside more traditionally defined diversity initiatives (such as those related to recruitment of staff): "by more intentionally incorporating social justice frameworks into common library functions such as information literacy education [and] research services [. . .] the academic library can do important work in achieving true social justice goals" (p. 6).

Incorporating social justice and critical pedagogy (a social movement that applies critical theory to education) into the instruction program will also prove useful for contributing to institutional assessment efforts in a progressive way:

> Keeping in mind that instruction program coordinators still must supply the evidence that institutions and accrediting organizations prefer—whether or not anyone will actually read it—the library instruction program's marginal position nonetheless provides it with a great opportunity to experiment with assessment practices and enact more critical methods that challenge the dominant modes of traditional assessment. (Accardi, 2010, p. 255)

Emphasizing critical information literacy or social pedagogy in the instruction program statement and purpose can provide many benefits, including a more inclusive teaching mission and alignment with equity, diversity, and inclusion efforts on campus. It also helps normalize these issues within the day-to-day work of librarians. The language used to incorporate these philosophies will likely depend on institutional context, but addressing these concepts in the instruction program statement sends a strong message about the goals and culture of the library's teaching and learning efforts.

The ACRL *Diversity Standards* (ACRL, 2012) note that when designing programs, academic libraries should focus on opportunities that are inclusive of the needs for all users; this demonstrates that the library has committed to upholding "cultural competence" by "ensuring equitable access to collections and library services" and "foster[ing] policies and procedures that [. . .] reflect varying cultural beliefs" (para. 34). Reviewing demographics of those that the instruction program serves (e.g., students and faculty), engaging stakeholders with a variety of perspectives in decision making, and advocating for an inclusive and equitable instruction program are important steps in the process of drafting an instruction program statement.

TURNING THE VISION INTO REALITY

Throughout the process of drafting and communicating the program statement, the Instruction Coordinator should remain true to the characteristics outlined in Chapter 1, namely intentionality and authenticity:

> The most important thing is that you, as the instruction coordinator, bring intention and strategy to the planning process. As with your teaching, improving your instruction program will be an iterative process where assessment and evaluation data let you know whether or not your program is headed in the right direction, and where your vision can help all of the instruction librarians on your team participate in enhancing and growing the program. (Benjes-Small & Miller, 2017, pp. 152–153)

While crucial for program alignment, and a necessary driver for assessment, the program statement, in many ways, is also a marketing tool. So how, then, does the Coordinator turn the instruction program statement and vision into reality? One important aspect is advocacy. This advocacy should be shared across the library; in other words, everyone is responsible for advancing and communicating the agenda of the instruction program. Having a strong and clear program statement will help guide that work. The next chapter explores how the program statement is necessary for effective and strong communication about the library's teaching and learning efforts.

Chapter Six

Advocating for an Instruction Program

MAKING THE CASE FOR INSTRUCTION

The previous chapter discussed the importance of having an instruction program statement; this high-level view of the program's mission and purpose is necessary not only for coordinating and guiding the efforts of teaching librarians but also for articulating the library's connection to the curriculum. How effective can the program statement be if it is not communicated clearly? Even if the statement is communicated clearly and often, is the right message reaching the right people? While it can seem like a never-ending job, advocating for a library instruction program is crucial. For Coordinators, advocacy may require stepping outside their comfort zone; as Bollman and Gallos (2011) assert, "good advocacy is complex. It is the ability to communicate clearly and persuasively. That means talking about your take on reality and the reasoning behind your diagnosis and decisions" (p. 45).

Academic librarians (and all librarians, in fact) are no strangers to advocacy efforts, as the thread of communicating value runs throughout all library workers' jobs. These efforts are particularly important for instruction librarians, who are often advocating their role as teaching partners across campus and, occasionally, in the library as well. The ACRL *Roles and Strengths* document cites "advocate" as one of the seven roles of teaching librarians, stating that advocacy:

> may involve persuasion, activism, encouragement, and support in many forms. A teaching librarian will need to be able to contextually situate information literacy and communicate its value across a range of audiences in the college/university community. Advocacy is required when working with library leaders and the college or university administration to promote and advance infor-

mation literacy, student learning, and the information literacy program within the overall library organization. (Amsberry et al., 2017, para. 11)

This chapter explores a variety of strategies for Instruction Coordinators involved in advocacy work for their instruction program (big or small), from identifying and engaging stakeholders to articulating the value of information literacy in both formal and informal instructional scenarios.

MARKETING AND PROMOTING THE INSTRUCTION PROGRAM

Before discussing the importance of identifying the stakeholders in library teaching advocacy efforts, it is worth taking a moment to discuss the always-present twin issues of *marketing* and *promotion*. This chapter focuses on the Coordinator as advocate of the instruction program, but this work can often get caught up in the equally important tasks of promoting and marketing the library's teaching services. While "promotion" is often used synonymously with "marketing," these two concepts accomplish slightly different purposes. Promotion is a smaller part of a bigger marketing plan; while Instruction Coordinators may indeed be involved in producing promotional materials for workshops, training, and available instructional services, these items are often still branded within the library's larger marketing strategy. Nims (1999) remarks that "having a person responsible for taking the pulse of library user needs and placing library instruction services in a context that is most beneficial for the use goes a long way to having a coherent and effective marking and promotion program" (p. 252). Where, then, does advocacy fit into this picture?

While information literacy librarians are key to communicating the value of an instruction program (Grassian & Kaplowitz, 2005), this role often falls primarily to the Instruction Coordinator; thus, this is where advocacy begins to play a bigger part. Promoting any library service is a two-way street, and Instruction Coordinators often sit at the intersection, advocating for and engaging with both librarians and administrators around the library's teaching and learning agenda. This internal advocacy may mean securing buy-in from teaching librarians and library administrators, or it could mean creating a more comprehensive communication plan for library colleagues. Coordinators face equally important, and sometimes more complex, advocacy scenarios outside of the library as well, often needing to serve as the primary spokesperson and advocate for the instruction program to the rest of campus. This should not be a solitary job, however, and strategies for engaging teaching librarians in advocacy efforts are shared next.

Crafting a Consistent Message

When developing any kind of promotional, marketing, or advocacy plans for the instruction program, Coordinators should talk with library communication or marketing units (if those exist), as well as other organizational stakeholders involved in outreach, research, or learning, to make sure the program is situated within the library's overall marketing structure and communication plan. Likewise, these goals should be explicitly tied to both the library's mission and vision statements, as well as the instruction program statement. Crafting a consistent, relevant message about the instruction program is crucial and will establish that the "message" is understood and communicated clearly by all library staff and administrators. Likewise, this will also ensure that the promotion and marketing goals for the instruction program are connected with the advocacy goals for the library's teaching and learning contributions. Coming up with a plan of action is an important part of this process. Often, this will mean boots-on-the-ground, person-to-person advocacy. In a study of information literacy librarians, Seymour (2012) found that "the most effective way to educate the university community about the library instruction program is individually through face-to-face communication" (pp. 60–61).

Advocacy Goals

Advocacy goals will vary, depending on both short- and long-term goals for both the instruction program and the library organization. Identifying metrics or benchmarks is a logical first step for Coordinators when planning program assessment (see the next chapter for a more thorough discussion of assessing instruction programs). The Instruction Program Advocacy Map (Advocacy Map) in Figure 6.1 will help in guiding the next steps. To facilitate brainstorming, consider these questions:

- Who are the constituents?
- What causes are important to them?
- What is the impact on student learning? On library services?

The Advocacy Map can be completed by the Coordinator alone, but should also be reviewed and discussed in conjunction with the program's teaching librarians; as previously mentioned, the more the librarians have buy-in and involvement in guiding the direction of the program, the more cohesive the program and its "message" will be—an important component for successful advocacy work.

The Advocacy Map (Figure 6.1) can also provide a foundation for guiding short- and long-term planning. As with any goal setting, Coordinators should take care to make sure the goals surrounding advocacy are "SMART"

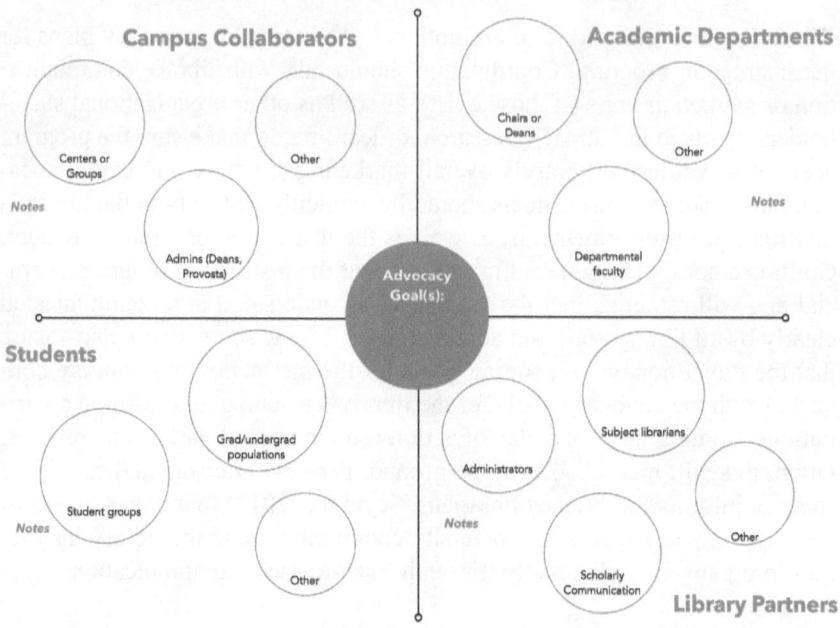

Figure 6.1. Instruction Program Advocacy Map. *Created by the author*

(specific, measurable, achievable, relevant, and timely); reflecting on and tying goals to the instruction program statement (discussed in the previous chapter) is crucial and will help set the stage for the assessment of the goals. One logical way to start planning for advocacy is to consider the partners and stakeholders related to the instruction program. A particular aspect to consider when determining advocacy partners is that teaching information literacy should be considered the job of many, rather than the job of a few:

> if it is assumed that everyone is taking some responsibility [for teaching information literacy], and that everyone in the academic community is charged with achieving these goals, it is more likely that no one person or subgroup will take specific responsibility and many skills that should be presented and practiced will fall through the cracks. (Hunt & Birks, 2004, p. 28)

The likelihood that information literacy instruction should extend beyond the instruction program makes it even more important for Coordinators to engage many constituents in any kind of promotion and marketing efforts.

ENGAGING STAKEHOLDERS

As discussed earlier in the book, identifying stakeholders is crucial for getting buy-in for library teaching and learning activities. Chapter 2 introduced some of the key players that Instruction Coordinators may want to engage with. This section provides additional context and strategies for developing internal (i.e., library-focused) and external (i.e., nonlibrary) partnerships. These collaborations are necessary to not only build an instruction program but also have implications for the growth and sustainability of a library's teaching efforts. The discussion begins with perhaps the most overlooked internal library stakeholders: the actual librarians who participate in the instruction program (both directly and indirectly).

Library Partners

Teaching Librarians

As previously discussed, the success of the instruction program is highly reliant on getting the teaching librarians on board with the program's vision. While it may seem a little obvious to consider teaching librarians as stakeholders, they are a unique group; for an instruction program to grow, develop, and sustain itself, having the primary contributors engaged in the visioning and advocacy of the department is crucial.

A considerable amount of time in this book has been spent already discussing the role of librarians as teachers. While Owusu-Ansah (2004) presents a point-counterpoint to the role of academic librarian as teacher, he ultimately urges that:

> librarians, always teaching, whether at the reference desk or in formal classroom settings, must accept formally their teaching role and engage actively in it, not sporadically, but as a generally accepted mandate of the profession and of the academic library in academe. (p. 16)

Not surprisingly, part of this acceptance also includes the willingness and initiative to promote the instruction program and advocate for themselves both in the classroom and out.

One strategy for engaging teaching librarians in promoting instruction is to encourage out-of-the-box thinking; as Galvin (2005) notes quite succinctly, "librarians cannot afford to overlook out-of-class opportunities to promote and support information literacy" (p. 352). Most academic librarians would agree that "teaching" and research support happen everywhere: the reference desk, librarians' offices, via online chat or video conferencing with students and faculty, and even on the sidewalk between buildings. Again, as Owusu-Ansah (2004) illustrates, these not-so-traditional methods of teaching take place all over campus (not just in the classroom), and the efforts to advocate for the library's role in cross-campus teaching should be shared by librarians throughout the library.

Library Administration

Another group that should appear on the Advocacy Map is library administration. Depending on where the instruction program fits within the greater library organizational chart, Instruction Coordinators will need to work closely with any number of administrators (e.g., Deans, Associate University Librarians, Directors, Department Heads). It is important for the Coordinator to develop a consistent mode of delivery for communicating the role of teaching and learning in the library; "managing up" in a sense, but also guiding library administrators by providing them with language for their own communication with faculty, campus administrators, and other high-level constituents.

Garnering administrative support is particularly important when the needs of the instruction program change. Perhaps, after an environmental scan, the Instruction Coordinator determines that the core mission of the program needs to shift. Or, due to institutional (e.g., strategic plans) or accreditation changes, the program's learning outcomes must be scrapped and redeveloped. In these cases, advocating for resources (e.g., time, positions) often falls to the Coordinator. When redeveloping the instruction program at Loyola Marymount University, Johnson-Grau, Archambault, Acosta, and McLean (2016) found administrative support to be crucial because it "recognized and rewarded librarian contributions and justified the commitment required to rebuild the entire information literacy program from scratch" (p. 753).

Academic Departments

Campus Administration

An important component of advocacy in all academic library work is building partnerships with campus administrators (Mallon, 2018). Whether engaging in strategic planning initiatives, supporting institutional accreditation efforts, or participating in programmatic assessment, by continually demonstrating value of the library in teaching and learning, the Coordinator is in a unique position to identify how the "big picture" of the instruction program can help the university achieve its goals. In particular, an instruction program that is flexible and responsive will likely garner more administrative support than one that refuses to adapt: "higher education is in a constant state of flux, and the more strategically aligned the library is, the easier it will be to make a case for critical infrastructure changes" (Mallon, 2018, p. 117). Staying attuned to institutional priorities related to accreditation and accountability can create opportunities for collaboration and advocacy for how the library can support these efforts. By tracking and taking advantage of institutional requirements, librarians can "actively participate in local efforts to define learning outcomes and demonstrate added value to student learning in response to these increasing calls for accountability" (Zald & Millet, 2012, p. 121).

Faculty

Faculty collaborations is a common theme throughout this book, as it will continue to be throughout the remaining chapters, because developing partnerships with faculty is one of the surest and, indeed, most necessary methods of incorporating information literacy into students' learning experiences.

One fairly obvious way to do this is to leverage existing partnerships. One might refer back to the information gathered when taking stock of the teaching climate on campus (see Chapter 2), or simply poll teaching librarians as to their "go to" advocates for the library's role in information literacy. Word of mouth can accomplish a lot, so when developing an advocacy plan, identifying those faculty and instructors with whom successful collaborations already exist will make things much easier. One must not lose hope if these partnerships are not already present; although it can take time to build lasting collaborations with faculty, the effort is worth it. Grassian and Kaplowitz (2005) recommend starting simply: "[instructional relationships] can start almost anywhere and any time with just a simple conversation about the changing landscape of information research [. . .] and the lack of critical thinking about information" exhibited by students (pp. 89–90). The Coordinator should be having these conversations with campus partners, but also encouraging teaching librarians to broach these subjects with faculty, as well.

Another way to identify and attract faculty advocates is by demonstrating the value of library instruction in assessing student learning. This connects to the previous conversation about accreditation and programmatic assessment, but it is also just as important in more focused environments like the classroom. While some faculty may not be surprised to learn that librarians have expertise in assignment design, and indeed are more than willing to grade research projects, it is still quite a surprise to many instructors. One reason for this may be because faculty members may have never experienced in-depth partnerships with librarians, or that their only experience with library instruction tended to be a one-shot session. The Instruction Coordinator should certainly advocate for the librarian's expertise in this area, but individual librarians need to push for these types of partnerships and consistently discuss assessment and data gathering with their faculty partners (Zald & Millet, 2012).

Other Campus Collaborators

It is important to note that library instruction efforts can (and most definitely should!) stretch beyond the academic curriculum. Just as curriculum mapping aligns information literacy instruction to departmental and program outcomes (more about this next), teaching and learning efforts can be mapped to co-curricular initiatives on campus, such as student success, athletics, or residential life. The ACRL *Roles and Strengths* document highlights the opportunity for librarians to engage in information literacy instruction beyond the classroom: "librarian leaders model instructional best practices as well as continuous learning and growth, facilitate the sharing of pedagogical ideas and experiences, and support teaching and learning efforts across disciplines and co-curricular areas" (Amsberry et al., 2017, para. 15).

Identifying other campus partners that also focus on student learning is a way to stretch the reach of an information literacy instruction program, whether through direct student instruction or via other methods. Librarians at Vanderbilt University, for example, found that collaborating with the Department of Athletics' Academic Support Center provided the perfect opportunity to approach information literacy instruction. Together they developed a train-the-trainer program for athletic counselors because: "given the counselors' regular contact with the student athletes, the librarians believed the counselors were in a position to reinforce the library's role in student success" (Costin & Morgan, 2019, p. 224).

Catching students in co-curricular environments is another influential way to advocate for the value of librarians and the development of digital, information, or other literacies. Although it can be difficult to identify the types and the frequency of student involvement in co-curricular activities, Lyle, Fournier, Phuwanartnurak, Lewis, and Roberts (2016) suggest that better communication among campus partners can increase the reach of co-curricular opportunities for students, particularly residential students. These partnerships will look different on every campus, depending on institutional size and organization. Some of the offices to investigate for advocacy efforts include those focusing on student learning and success (e.g., academic affairs; advising; or residential and campus life), as well as those focusing on faculty development and teaching (e.g., centers for teaching; instructional designers; or an educational technologies/digital learning department). Campus partners can also rely on one another for promoting research workshops and other instructional programming (Lyle, Fournier, Phuwanartnurak, Lewis, & Roberts, 2016).

Students

Academic library instruction programs have a diverse audience, which includes many of the stakeholders mentioned earlier. However, when it comes to advocacy, the primary audience for library instruction is often overlooked: students! Librarians continuously advocate *for* students, but how often do librarians advocate the importance of library instruction *to* students? This may be because students are a fairly captive audience; they are often required to attend library instruction sessions, whether because the instruction is integrated into their courses, or there is some other incentive for them to attend a research skills workshop (e.g., academic requirements for athletes or within the Greek system). Academic libraries spend a lot of time analyzing and assessing students' needs and then advocating to faculty for how library instruction can meet these needs, but perhaps more needs to be done to address instructional services for students as learners, not just as a captive audience.

Curtis (2016) encourages librarians to consider students as peer-to-peer information literacy advocates, as well; by engaging in teaching information literacy skills to their peers, students can develop a higher level of confidence and communication of research skills. This strategy of peer-to-peer advocacy can similarly be utilized for word-of-mouth growth of the information literacy program; for example, Instruction Coordinators can engage library student workers to share the value of meeting with subject librarians to discuss research projects. Students that have already met with librarians in previous classes can be encouraged to (gently) persuade new instructors of the value of having an instruction librarian embedded in the course curriculum.

The ACRL Instruction Section's (2018) *Research Agenda for Library Instruction and Information Literacy* recommends several guiding questions to assist in creating "meaningful educational environments and enduring library instruction programs that meet an individual's current and future needs as a student and lifelong learner:

1. How can the emergence of new campus audiences have an impact on academic library instruction?
2. How can instruction programs best recognize and adapt to changes in the characteristics of and variety of targeted audiences?
3. What issues should librarians be aware of for marketing and promotion, and outreach to these groups?
4. How might the type, timing, and location of instruction be best tailored to each audience?
5. Conversely, how can learning objects be reused for multiple audiences without compromising learning?" (para. 5–6)

These questions can assist Coordinators in reflecting on their advocacy efforts with the student body, particularly on issues related to diversity and complexity of student experience. That reflection can then guide instruction program development.

CURRICULUM MAPPING

Information literacy curriculum mapping (ILCM), introduced in Chapter 2, aligns the instruction programs' outcomes and priorities to that of the curriculum. Curriculum mapping is an extremely effective method of communicating value to stakeholders, as noted by Charles (2015):

> today's academic environment presents an opportunity for the creation and implementation of an ILCM that is aligned with discipline specific content, tools, and research methods and is integrated into coursework so as to demonstrate value to students. Also, the librarian-faculty partnerships can demonstrate to students that their instructors endorse research instruction. Moreover, if learning outcomes directly address research skills and appear in the syllabus, students will see research and IL as an integral part of the course and this may diffuse any apathy on their part. Implementation of an ILCM is an opportunity to address all of these concerns at the undergraduate level. (p. 49)

Booth, Brecher, Lowe, Stone, and Tagge (2014) provide a large number of disciplinary curriculum maps (a template is available at http://bit.ly/ccl-template), created using an online concept mapping tool. Creating digital curriculum maps will allow for multiple collaborators (e.g., the Instruction Coordinator, subject librarians, faculty, or library administrators), and is more conducive to an iterative model. As Archambault and Masunaga (2015) reflect, curriculum mapping "helps answer the question of what the place is for information literacy in the curriculum as a whole" (p. 516).

Curriculum mapping is a crucial exercise for program development and advocacy, as it helps define and express indented results of the instruction program (Hinchliffe, 2016b). Buchanan, Webb, Houk, and Tingelstad (2015) also note that curriculum mapping "allows participants to clearly articulate their intended outcomes and visually evaluate how those outcomes fit into the student experience" and "allows librarians to see how their intentions match with reality and to plan for the future" (p. 97). To be the most strategically effective, Archambault and Masunaga (2015) suggest that maps use shared language (with academic programs), align with disciplinary information literacy concepts or standards, and have clearly communicated goals. In particular, articulating the curriculum map's goals to stakeholders, as suggested by Charles (2015), provides a visual demonstration of value, and sets the stage for assessment of academic programs as well as the library's instruction program.

COMMUNICATING VALUE

Coordinators are often responsible for communicating the value of an instruction program to multiple stakeholder groups. Identifying priorities and internal goals for each group will help in crafting the message for advocacy efforts, so it may take some research and information gathering to identify what will resonate with each group of constituents. Zald and Millet (2012) found that some faculty, for instance, respond well to comparative assessment data about students' research skills, and are more likely to agree that information literacy instruction is important when students' research and critical thinking skill levels fall below that of peer institutions. Library administration will also likely respond to data-driven arguments, so consulting benchmarks supplied by the Association of Research Libraries, the Association of College and Research Libraries, or regional accrediting agencies can be useful resources to gather.

University administrators will also have their own, usually much loftier and bigger picture priorities, and it is important to remember that these priorities will often change fairly quickly. Weiner (2012) reminds librarians to first consider the characteristics and makeup of the university when planning advocacy efforts to communicate the value of the library's role in teaching and learning:

> according to how effective communication occurs, which campus relationships should be developed and how, what institutional knowledge should be invoked, whether incentives and awards are helpful, what publicity is important, how power should be used, and what processes are important. Those who want to institutionalize information literacy need to have the ability to identify the organizational norms and preferences of their institution and plan accordingly. (p. 291)

Several strategies for laying this groundwork and identifying institutional characteristics (particularly concerning the culture of teaching and learning) are discussed in more detail in Chapters 2 and 3.

AN ADVOCATE'S WORK IS NEVER DONE

Wendy Newman, Senior Fellow and Lecturer in the Faculty of Information at the University of Toronto (as quoted in Lankes [2016]), eloquently sums up the importance of advocacy in libraries:

librarianship is steeped in community, and [. . .] advocacy is all about relationships. Great librarianship and great advocacy are not about the survival of libraries as institutions, or indeed about any institutions, but about the improvement of society [. . .] competence in advocacy entails both advocating for the community and helping others become advocates. Enter librarians as advocates because it's not enough for us to carry out the work of librarianship without continuously and intentionally engaging the support that's necessary. (pp. 85–86)

While Newman's comments are about libraries in general, it is not a far stretch to make the same argument about the library's role in teaching and learning in higher education. By the nature of their positions, Instruction Coordinators are central to this argument: their advocacy runs across many levels and involves a fairly consistent and high level of not only being an individual advocate, but also in coaching their colleagues to share in advocacy efforts.

The next chapter explores the ever-present need for assessing the instruction program. While each layer of program development, revision, and growth needs consistent review, evaluating the efforts of advocacy concerning the teaching and learning program is essential in making sure teaching efforts are in line with stakeholder expectations and priorities. Updating the Instruction Program Advocacy Map annually, or even term by term, can help Coordinators be at the ready to change gears and revise the message or focus of the instruction program, as dictated by internal and external guidance.

Chapter Seven

Assessing an Instruction Program

DEVELOPING A CYCLE OF ASSESSMENT

The previous chapter focused on the importance of advocating for and marketing an instruction program and the specific role the Instruction Coordinator has to play in this advocacy, but what happens when things do not go as planned? What happens when the instruction program is not meeting its goals, when it does not live up to its program statement, or when teaching librarians veer off course from the rest of their team? This is when the assessment of the instruction program is crucially important. If not for the cycle of continuous revision and consistent updating of services and programs, the instruction program would become outdated and lose relevance very quickly. Teaching librarians are no strangers to assessment; they have devised many ways to creatively and authentically assess student learning, both in individual sessions and across multiple courses and programs. This assessment of student learning is crucial, not only for communicating the importance and value of having a library teaching and learning program but also for informing the pedagogical practices of instruction librarians. However, student learning assessment is only one part of the bigger picture of the success of the instruction program and, inevitably, it often falls to the Instruction Coordinator to identify how learning assessment fits into the larger picture of the achievement and reach of the library's teaching and learning offerings. The ACRL *Guidelines* (2011), which have been referenced multiple times already within this book, state that assessment of instruction programs is a crucial and "systematic ongoing [process] that inform[s] and guide[s] Library strategic direction" (ACRL, 2011).

A FEW CLARIFICATIONS

Before going further, it might be helpful to differentiate between the terms *assessment* (in particular, *program assessment*) and *evaluation*, which are often mistakenly used interchangeably. **Program assessment** is the systematic and ongoing method of gathering, analyzing, and using information from various sources about a program and measuring program outcomes. **Evaluation**, on the other hand, typically refers to appraising or reviewing a process, thing, or person (e.g., annual performance evaluations or instructor course evaluations). Evaluations are used for process improvement and can play an important role in the growth of an instruction program; for example, student evaluations of instruction sessions can help librarians gain insight into their teaching, as well as provide the Coordinator with valuable feedback in working with the librarians in their program. However, program assessment is about much more than these evaluatory methods.

An additional point of clarification is related to student learning assessment: as mentioned, student assessment is an integral part of the work of instruction librarians, and it would be hard to talk about assessing an instruction program without a discussion of student learning. According to Angelo (1995),

> Assessment [. . .] involves making our expectations explicit and public; setting appropriate criteria and high standards for learning quality; systematically gathering, analyzing, and interpreting evidence to determine how well performance matches those expectations and standards; and using the resulting information to document, explain, and improve performance. When it is embedded effectively within larger institutional systems, assessment can help us focus our collective attention, examine our assumptions, and create a shared academic culture dedicated to assuring and improving the quality of higher education. (p. 7)

As Angelo (1995) notes, assessment of student learning can be used to inform and guide the teaching and learning efforts of an institution or program. While that is an important piece of the puzzle (and will be discussed more next), this chapter focuses on assessing *the success of the instruction program itself*. This includes student learning, but also the other aspects of a successful instruction program, such as resources, spaces, staffing, and technology. This programmatic assessment is necessary for identifying the pedagogical impact of the library's teaching and learning efforts (what is working? where are the gaps?), advocating for resource allocation, and informing strategic direction. When analyzing the success of an instruction program, Zald and Gilchrist (2008) suggest a holistic view of academic assessment that includes "assessment of student learning, assessment of the value and contributions of the information literacy instruction program, and assessment of the teaching contributions and growth of individual librarians" (p. 165). In addition to program-level outcomes, the assessment plan (discussed shortly) should also include consistent and timely review and analysis of the many resources allocated to instructional efforts, which could include budget, technology, staffing, teaching spaces, and more. With the focus of this book on library instruction programs, in particular, this chapter presents considerations and strategies for Instruction Coordinators to programmatically assess the library's teaching and learning efforts as well as the strength of the overall program.

A Note on Program Goals and Outcomes

Assessing outcomes in the context of program review can be confusing since instruction librarians so often think in terms of outcomes centered around student learning. Assessment plans, which are discussed shortly, should include measurable outcomes tied to program goals. To help differentiate this work from student learning assessment, an additional point of clarification is necessary. When writing program-level outcomes, it can be tempting to focus on only those that deal with student learning. To help with this differentiation, think about session-level outcomes as those that are focused on the learning that is to take place as a result of the instruction; these are often tied to course or discipline-specific information literacy skills. For example, an instruction session for a psychology research methods course might include the learning outcome: *as a result of the instruction, students will be able to describe basic research methods in psychology research, including research design, data analysis, and interpretation.* The librarian teaching the session should be able to assess whether or not this outcome was achieved through formative or summative assessment measures. On a higher level, however, there are the program outcomes; these are the goals and outcomes that are directly aligned with the instruction program statement, and, when assessed, demonstrate whether or not the instruction program is meeting its stated purpose. The ACRL *Standards for Libraries in Higher Education* (ACRL *Standards for Libraries*) (2018) provide several sample outcomes focusing on the library's educational role (Principle 3 in the ACRL *Standards for Libraries*). These outcomes, which are based on stated performance indicators, can provide guidance for the outcomes-based assessment of the instruction program. Sample outcomes that may be useful include, but are not limited to, the following:

- Faculty seek the input of librarians on the use of library resources in the course and assignment development.
- Students use library collections for both curricular and co-curricular information needs.

- Faculty require students to use a variety of sources from library databases.
- Faculty seek the input of librarians in developing information literacy learning outcomes for their courses and assignments.
- Librarians design and administer information literacy instruction sessions that incorporate hands-on, active learning techniques. (ACRL, 2018, pp. 16–17)

Again, the program-level outcomes provide the Coordinator with concrete evidence that will assist in measuring the success of the instruction program.

ASSESSING THE INSTRUCTION PROGRAM

Before jumping into what constitutes "success" for an individual instruction program, it can be useful to delve further into what exactly is meant by "program assessment." The introduction to this chapter touches on the nuances between evaluation and assessment, but what does it mean to assess an instruction program, and why is it important? Colborn and Cordell (1998) note that:

> program assessment of a library's instruction offerings means an overall analysis of the effect of library instruction on the learning of the institution's students. This is rarely done because there are no perfect measures, and there is relatively little reward for undertaking such an enormous task [. . .] the ideal definition of program assessment would be the analysis of the library's effect on students' learning of information literacy skills. (p. 126)

The difficulty in assessing an instruction program, as noted by Colborn and Cordell (1998), is not lost; it can indeed be a daunting task, particularly if one is undertaking an assessment of the overall program for the first time. Thankfully, there are documents available to help guide Coordinators in the programmatic assessment. The ACRL *Guidelines* recommend that the following aspects should be considered when assessing a library instruction program:

- Measures [. . .] based on specific a) student learning outcomes and b) overall program goals;
- A variety of indirect and direct measures assessing various aspects of the program, for example, needs assessment, participant reaction, teaching effectiveness, overall effectiveness of program;
- Regular data collection and analysis using such measures;
- Periodic revision of program based on data analysis;
- A feedback loop that assesses the sustainability of the program; and

- Coordination of assessment with library administration and teaching faculty where appropriate. (ACRL, 2011)

Likewise, the ACRL *Characteristics of Programs of Information Literacy* lay out several expectations for instruction program assessment:

- Follows a process for program planning, evaluation, and revision;
- Measures progress toward meeting program goals and objectives;
- Integrates with the course and curriculum assessment, institutional evaluations and regional and professional accreditation initiatives; and
- Uses appropriate assessment/evaluation methods for relevant purposes, for example, formative, summative, short-term or longitudinal. (ACRL, 2019)

In addition to consulting and incorporating the aforementioned guiding professional statements, Instruction Coordinators will also want to think about the model or framework in which their program is situated, particularly when assessing the student learning piece. This framework should provide the foundation for all instruction program assessment, just as it guides the instruction program statement, and influences the content development, goals, and objectives for the instruction program. No matter what the foundation upon which the instruction program sits (e.g., the ACRL *Framework*, signature pedagogies, or one of the other models discussed in Chapter 4), there will exist some built-in methods for assessment that lend themselves to the chosen framework. Assessment methods and tools such as rubrics, peer assessment or feedback, librarians' self-reflections, data on student academic success, curriculum mapping, and teaching portfolios are all strategies that can be developed around the ACRL *Framework* or other models (Bowles-Terry, 2012; Chapman, Pettway, & White, 2001; Gerwitz, 2014). For example, an instruction program's teaching portfolio (i.e., a collection of all librarians' lesson plans, learning outcomes, reflections, and data on student learning) can "serve as a written legacy of an instruction program" and guide future assessment efforts (Chapman, Pettway, & White, 2001, p. 295). Additionally, Tancheva, Andrews, and Steinhart (2007) recommend attitudinal surveys, which can be particularly useful for gathering stakeholder feedback, which is discussed more next.

THE ASSESSMENT PLAN

While there are several templates and resources available for assessing various academic programs, there are not quite as many established methods or "plans" for assessing library instruction or information literacy programs (although quite a few homegrown examples can be found via an internet search). However, almost all the suggestions for nonlibrary academic program assessment are transferable and will help Instruction Coordinators think more holistically about program assessment, which can be a difficult task, especially for those who are used to thinking about assessment primarily in terms of individual class sessions.

The components of a successful assessment plan mirror many of the requirements for program development that have been touched on through the early chapters of this book (and will be discussed in more detail in the final chapters). The following is a list of commonly recommended steps or sections to include in an assessment plan (College of Business Administration, 2016; Stassen et al., 2001):

- A program statement
- Measurable learning outcomes and program goals
- Curriculum maps (optional, but common in library instruction program assessment)
- A method for gathering data or evidence
- A plan to analyze and interpret findings
- Venues for disseminating the findings

As all experienced educators know, assessment is cyclical; there is no "end point" to assessing an instruction program. Each of the components of an assessment plan should be regularly evaluated for relevance and currency and checked for alignment with the instruction program statement, bigger picture library goals and mission, and institutional priorities. A strategy for Instruction Coordinators that are trying to maintain a regular cycle of assessment while tackling other duties is to determine which measures of success are most important to the instruction program and develop assessment techniques that provide benchmarks and metrics.

MEASURES OF SUCCESS

Coordinators may find it extremely difficult to measure the impact of teaching and learning at all, much less the instruction program as a whole; one strategy for approaching this is to identify what success looks like for the instruction program. These metrics should be goal-oriented and explicitly tied to the instruction program statement. Referring back to the environmental scan (see Chapter 2) can provide guideposts for who and what is important to the instruction program. The following section offers several components by which the Coordinator can both analyze and measure the success of their program. After examining the possible measures of success, several options for data collection to aid in program assessment are discussed.

Benchmarking

A good place to start when identifying measures of success for an assessment plan is benchmarking. Benchmarking, which is a "mechanism for comparative analysis of the efficiency of one company with the performance of other, more successful" entities (Rzheuskyi & Kunanets, 2018, p. 45), is crucial for helping illustrate program success. The benefits of benchmarking are numerous (Epper, 1999; McClenney, 2006). Not only does benchmarking provide a contextual starting point for data collection, the practice is also crucial for identifying gaps in the overall teaching efforts that can indicate areas of improvement or renewed focus. Additionally, engaging in collaborative benchmarking (i.e., the Instruction Coordinator and the teaching librarians) strengthens the culture of teaching and learning and helps build a collective mindset for continuous improvement.

Rzheuskyi and Kunanets (2018) note that while there is not an established methodology for benchmarking in library science, it should nevertheless "be used for comparative analysis of the investigated library institute with the library-leader selected as a standard for the purpose of borrowing work experience and its use to improve the efficiency of the library institute" (p. 45). St. Clair (2006) finds benchmarking to be an effective strategy for strategic planning and assessment, and notes that "process benchmarking" in particular is useful for examining "the [program's] workflow to help a planning unit improve its effectiveness and/or efficiency" (para. 2). St. Clair (2006) recommends developing process benchmarks for program assessment because "they (1) specify a best practice that is clearly superior to local practice and (2) provide a clear direction for implementing it into the local organization" (para. 8). The *ACRL Guidelines* (ACRL, 2011) recommends some external benchmarking areas, such as:

- measurable program learning outcomes
- learning assessment plans or curriculum maps
- institutional alignment of information literacy skills
- educational technologies and spaces
- appropriate pedagogical professional development for librarians
- collaborations with campus units on teaching and learning

This type of benchmarking can be a particularly useful strategy for libraries that are in the initial stages of assessing the instruction program, as benchmarking provides a baseline for demonstrating growth. Internal benchmarks will focus on central factors relating to the specific library and the instruction program; for example, number of sessions, number of students taught, or embedded teaching partnerships. Internal benchmarking can also measure the reach of the instruction program and the program's outcomes regarding issues relating to student retention or job placement. While benchmarking against peer library and instruction programs (using national data on peer institutions, pulled from entities such as ACRL or the Association of Research Libraries) will provide much-needed data comparison points, Coordinators will most definitely want to engage in this internal benchmarking.

Benchmarking is not without its challenges, however. One danger is that the process of benchmarking can create a false sense of security in terms of what a program is doing well in; as Freiling and Huth (2005) note, "the objects which are observed in a benchmarking process are very often not much more than the 'tip of an iceberg'" (p. 4). This is particularly salient when comparing one's program to external peers, because of the vast differences in instruction programs. While aggregated data on peer instruction program outcomes, number of sessions, or learning assessments can be useful in setting aspirational goals, this data often fails to include information about the resources allocated to the programs, the number of librarians teaching information literacy classes, or other factors such as budget or space. This can result in a false equivalency that makes these benchmarks nearly impossible to reach. Internal benchmarking can also be challenging, particularly when the benchmarking is comparing librarians at the same institution. This can result in an unhealthy competition, which is counter to fostering the inclusive teaching and learning climate discussed in Chapter 3. Acknowledging and addressing these challenges can aid in the use of benchmarking as a successful method for instruction program assessment.

Student Learning Assessment

Not surprisingly, a primary method for assessing the impact of the instruction program is to measure the impact of the library's teaching efforts on student learning. Of course, learning that takes place in one class does not indicate programmatic success on a larger scale. The Coordinator should develop clear and measurable learning outcomes for the instruction program; this will, in turn, guide the instructional design process and contextualize teaching within the larger organizational and institutional framework. In other words, what should teaching librarians accomplish? What should the program accomplish? Working backwards in this way can be stymying, but design strategies that encourage a holistic view of teaching can make this task easier. Kinzie, Hutchings, and Jankowski (2015) note that the backward-design approach, although most often used for designing classroom instruction, can also be used at a broader scale, as long as it is tied to learning outcomes: "once [the outcomes] are determined, instruction and practice that support them as well as evidence that demonstrates them are identified with the purpose of facilitating students' movement toward the outcomes" (p. 63).

Table 7.1 shows several sample instruction program outcomes that can provide the basis for assessment, some of which are aligned with the ACRL *Framework*. The University of Arizona Libraries (UAL), for example, identified learning outcomes that they "believe best meet our campus learning and teaching needs" (Pagowsky, 2019). The UAL are somewhat famous for doing away with one-shot library instruction, in part to create a more authentic and relevant information literacy experience for students, but also for easier assessment and more scaffolded learning: "we use assessment to tell a story about our instruction program, and look at both qualitative and quantitative information; and we use curriculum mapping to visualize how information literacy fits into the curriculum and where it is most effective" (Pagowsky, 2019). Typically, these program-level learning outcomes can also be modified by teaching librarians to guide assessment at the session/course and/or departmental level. One important note is that not all of the examples in Table 7.1 are tied to information literacy skills. Depending on the focus and scope of the instruction program, the learning outcomes may be more broad and reference other concepts related to lifelong learning, digital literacy, aspects of the research process, or, as in the case of Dickinson College, concepts related to pedagogy and professional development of teaching librarians (which provides a good example of program outcomes that expand beyond student learning).

Table 7.1. Sample Instruction Program Learning Outcomes

Dickinson College Libraries	• Assess local information literacy practice to improve existing programs and create opportunities for new ones • Collaborate with appropriate constituents to create the best information literacy learning environment for students and foster lifelong learning • Increase awareness among faculty, students and administrators of information literacy and its benefits and importance to academic success • Train librarians in best practices for teaching and assessing information literacy skill sets (Program Goals, n.d.)
Portland State University	• Select appropriate means for recording or saving relevant sources to retrieve them when needed • Examine a work's citation and abstract to determine its relevance to their research • Recognize issues related to privacy, ethics, intellectual property and copyright to respect the rights of others, comply with laws and contracts, or safeguard personal information (Portland State University Library, n.d.)
University of Arizona Libraries	• Identify the contribution of specific scholarly pieces and varying perspectives to a disciplinary knowledge conversation • Formulate research questions based on curiosity and gaps in information or data available • Critique and evaluate information to contribute to the construction of knowledge and make it stronger • Identify scholarly publication practices and how they provide and/or hinder access to scholarly information (Pagowsky, 2019)
University of Southern California Libraries	• Debate the ways privilege influences perception of authority • Recognize that similar content may be presented in different formats, which may affect the interpretation of the content • Give credit to the original ideas of others through attribution and/or formal conventions • Select research methodology(ies) based on need, circumstance, and type of inquiry • Describe the way that systems privilege some perspectives and present barriers to others • Design searches strategically, considering and selecting systems to search and evaluate search results (USC Libraries, n.d.)

Again, the instruction program statement is crucial for guiding the development of program-level learning outcomes. This process is made even stronger when defining program outcomes is a collaborative and inclusive effort between the Instruction Coordinator and the teaching librarians; as Benjes-Small and Miller (2017) note:

> Defining the scope of the group's work is a first step that will allow you to assess student learning and evaluate the program. [. . .] many instruction programs define programmatic outcomes that identify the specific areas of student learning with which the instruction program engages. These top-level outcomes help you create boundaries for your team's work, and also can help you to define the areas in which you need to gather evidence for assessment and evaluation purposes. (p. 155)

Strategic Alignment

Outcomes assessment can also help guide other measures of success, such as strategic alignment of the instruction program. The importance of alignment has been discussed previously (particularly in regard to strategic plans and accreditation efforts), but one sure way of expressing the impact of the library's teaching and learning efforts is by showing how the instruction program helps meet goals of both the larger library organization and the institution.

Bowles-Terry (2012) touches on the importance of university curriculum-wide learning outcomes to aid in programmatic assessment of information literacy; typically, library instruction programs have lacked "common guidelines for librarians to teach information literacy with increasing complexity; however, in the future with [a] common set of practices, we may know with more certainty which skills students have learned and at what level of study" (p. 83). This information can be used to align the program's goals with strategic plans, external mission statements, institutional review guidelines, and accreditation policies. According to Kuh et al. (2015), "external entities—especially accreditors, but also federal and state governments, philanthropic organizations, and higher education associations—should emphasize the use of results and the impact of changes in policies and practices on learning outcomes and institutional culture" (p. 9). By ensuring alignment of the instruction program with these policies, the Instruction Coordinator will be able to more clearly articulate the value and purpose of program assessment.

Program Statement Alignment and Programmatic Expectations

Whereas the other measures of success listed are somewhat subjective and theoretically less defined, the instruction program's statement is an established and (ideally) agreed-upon document that should guide the program's activities and goal setting. During the assessment cycle, one of the most important things a Coordinator should review is components and goals established from the program statement; in other words, are the objectives that drove the creation of the program statement being met? For example, if the program statement includes principles of Universal Design for Learning (UDL), was it a success? Why or why not?

If there is any dissatisfaction or indication that the goals and objectives of the program statement are *not* being met or satisfied, then it is likely time to review the statement and perhaps even rewrite it. Outcomes assessment can help indicate whether or not the objectives are being met, or if there is a gap in mission between the Coordinator and the teaching librarians. Using the sample outcomes in the ACRL *Standards for Libraries* (2018) as a guidepost can also help with the outcomes assessment. For example, if an instruction program has an outcome stating *"Librarians design and administer information literacy instruction sessions that incorporate hands-on, active learning techniques,"* the Coordinator would need to determine what it would mean to achieve this outcome. Perhaps a certain percentage of instruction sessions should include active learning techniques each semester. Or, the program could have a goal charging librarians to incorporate at least one new active learning or formative assessment technique per semester (this is an easily measurable goal). Knowing what success looks like for each of these program outcomes allows the Coordinator to assess current efforts and will guide future plans, as well. It will also allow the Coordinator to advocate for more resources, when appropriate.

The program statement, while serving as a living document, is an explicit and agreed upon statement that can be used for measuring the success of the program. However, what about the more implicit goals and hopes for the program? Chapter 3 introduces the importance of building and fostering a culture of teaching and learning in the library. The Coordinator may feel that things are going well, but do the teaching librarians feel the same way? Are they still engaged and active in the mission of the program, or are they simply going through the motions? How satisfied are library administrators with the instruction program (anecdotally or driven by data)? These questions definitely verge into the territory of "evaluation"—but are an important part of determining the overall success of the program.

Stakeholder Feedback

Another measure of success (again, not surprisingly) is stakeholder feedback. Without repeating the many stakeholders of an instruction program, readers should be reminded that these constituents are likely to be different for each library and each program, and the list will often change. Because of this, reviewing the list of stakeholders and getting their feedback as part of the program assessment cycle is important and must occur on a regular basis. Whether they realize it or not, all stakeholders likely have their own expectations for the program (just as the Instruction Coordinator does); teaching librarians, administrators, students, and others can also guide the future direction of the program and provide much needed check-ins to make sure things are moving along intentionally and smoothly. These check-ins also allow the Coordinator to ensure that the instruction program is meeting its goals for the different stakeholder groups, as set out in the initial planning stages of program development. Each group will provide unique and varied feedback. For example, a Coordinator can track how the library has helped with assessing student learning in relation to accreditation requirements. Perhaps the library has collaborated with co-curricular campus partners such as the writing studio or the career center to teach targeted research skills. Are these partners seeing an improvement in student learning? Are appropriate resources allocated to these partnerships? Asking these guiding questions can help the Coordinator assess the instruction program's impact. Other environmental factors that can be evaluated on a regular basis include resources and space allocation for instruction activities and library collections that support pedagogical and professional development of teaching librarians and others in the library and university that directly support teaching, learning, and research.

DATA COLLECTION

The goals for program assessment will guide the type of evidence and data that will help assess the measures of success identified above. Although this was touched upon earlier, it is worth stressing again: while assessment of student learning in individual instruction sessions (even in a scaffolded program) is crucial to the success of an instruction program, these efforts cannot be viewed in isolation. Rather, the Instruction Coordinator must look at *all* learning assessment to see how it fits into the picture of the library's overall teaching initiatives.

The Scholarship of Teaching and Learning (SoTL) can frame the conversation with librarians about overall program assessment. Particularly if the Coordinator has developed a SoTL Community of Practice and/or normalized SoTL research (as suggested in Chapter 3) as an integral part of the teaching and learning culture in the library, librarians may already be familiar with SoTL work, thus making it a bit easier to frame the discussion of data collection related to instruction program assessment. Many of the strategies used for designing SoTL research projects in the classroom (i.e., at the micro level) are transferable to the meso (departmental) or even macro (institutional) levels. As Miller-Young et al. (2017) comment, "even those who do not conduct their own SoTL projects are consumers of SoTL who apply the knowledge produced by its scholars in their teaching, curriculum development, or program reviews" (p. 8). Hutchings's (2000) SoTL taxonomy, particularly the "What is?" and "What works?" questions, can also provide a guidepost for framing program assessment.

Methodologies such as longitudinal design or phenomenography can provide useful ways of thinking about program assessment, as well. Common qualitative data collection methods, such as focus groups and interviews, are also good ways of engaging multiple stakeholders. For example, are library administrators satisfied with the amount and depth of information literacy sessions? The Instruction Coordinator can focus on higher level stakeholders (e.g., deans and program administrators) as well as the instruction librarians that make up the program, while the librarians might focus on faculty, department chairs, and students. Students, in particular, can also play an integral part in data collection; Kinzie, Hutchings, and Jankowski (2015) suggest having students run focus groups with their peers, as well as analyze both quantitative and qualitative data that may be gathered by formative assessment methods.

While it may be tempting to rely on evaluation instruments (e.g., "did this instruction session positively impact your confidence in doing research?"), instruction librarians and Coordinators should be wary of using these instruments for program assessment; instead, they should take the time to determine whether or not these types of evaluative methods are actually providing useful data that will positively impact the future direction of the instruction program. Zald and Gilchrist (2008) provide some background, and caution, on information gathering that is solely evaluative in nature:

> For librarians, evaluations have been a common way to elicit feedback about instruction. Evaluations generally focused on student or faculty opinion regarding the qualities of the librarian or usefulness of the session. This approach developed within an assessment context associated with accountability; one that considered administrative needs more than those of the learning enterprise. The emphasis has now shifted to focus on student learning outcomes, and the real value of assessment in this context is the clarity it provides for students, librarians, and faculty [. . .] the goal of assessment is not to achieve a particular score from student assignments, but instead to determine what we can learn in order to increase our effectiveness as teachers. (p. 165)

Occasionally, Instruction Coordinators are required by administrators to provide this type of data as part of regular assessment reports, but library administrators should also encourage the Coordinators or directors of their instruction programs to develop a more comprehensive look at the impact of the program by collating and analyzing both qualitative evaluations and authentic student learning data. When presented side by side, these two sets of evidence can denote *success* of the teaching that occurs, while also illustrating learning and growth.

Finally, it is also important to consider factors related to how data will be analyzed and used/disseminated. Those leading instruction programs should be familiar with student data policies, such as Institutional Review Board (IRB) and FERPA compliance, and should take care to ensure any data collection is run through and approved by these campus entities (particularly if it is meant for dissemination outside of the library).

KEEPING THE BIGGER PICTURE IN MIND

As with many aspects of planning and directing an instruction program, assessment of that program must be part of the bigger picture. The Instruction Coordinator has an important and crucial role in assuring that the instruction program will:

> establish, assess, and link academic library outcomes to institutional outcomes related to the following areas: student enrollment, student retention and graduation rates, student success, student achievement, student learning, student engagement, faculty research productivity, faculty teaching, service, and overarching institutional quality. (Oakleaf, 2010, p. 12)

This may seem like a complicated and overwhelming task, but by creating an assessment plan and knowing what success looks like (and how it can be measured) can make the experience a little less daunting. Coordinators should also remember that they do not need to tackle programmatic assessment on their own; there are a number of partners in the library and on campus that can help—instruction librarians, assessment coordinators, institutional research offices, centers for teaching, and even data scientists are all powerful resources for planning, gathering, analyzing, and disseminating program assessment data.

Castro Gessner and Eldemire (2015) very succinctly articulate the underlying purpose and importance of an instruction program assessment plan: "besides communicating the value of academic librarians to the teaching mission of the institution, a program-level assessment plan helps to manage library teaching staff efficiently and effectively" (p. 5). The next chapter delves into the inevitable moment when things go astray, posing several questions for re-engaging with the measures of success listed above, as well as strategies for framing the (also inevitable, but perhaps more daunting) task of moving forward.

Chapter Eight

When an Instruction Program Goes Astray

WHAT IT MEANS TO "GO ASTRAY"

After taking stock of an existing program, developing a program statement, supporting and growing librarians as teachers, fostering a culture of teaching and learning in the library, promoting and advocating for the instruction program, and incorporating evidence from assessment and evaluation, it seems like an Instruction Coordinator's work should be finished. However, the "set it and forget it" mindset is a poor fit for dynamic academic institutions and the ever-changing research and information landscape. To be successful in the long term, an instruction program must evolve and adapt in ways that are aligned with its library and its institution. Otherwise, the program will stand still, or go astray.

Simply put, an instruction program that has gone astray does not work as well as it used to. This can become apparent on the micro level, with low attendance in individual workshops or lack of interest from specific faculty partners. Or, it may be an issue on the macro level, with library instruction that is out of sync with the mainstream of teaching and learning at the institution or higher education in general. Grassian and Kaplowitz (2005) cite "potential [information literacy]-related problems" that can occur among teaching librarians, including "conviction that there is a *right way* to teach"; "poor communication skills with instructors, colleagues, and administrators"; and, "lack of sensitivity to learners' feelings" (p. 75). They also identify attitudes of administrators that may signal more systemic instruction program issues, such as a "lack of trust in [instruction] librarians' individual teaching styles"; "playing the numbers game by pressing for more and more in-person instruction to boost statistics"; and, "always striving for the next new thing"

(Grassian & Kaplowitz, 2005, p. 75). The program itself may be successful, but the teaching librarians within it may suffer from burnout or low morale, struggle with workplace conflict, or drift away from the program's mission due to lack of cohesion within the team. Any of these issues may arise suddenly, or they may creep in over time. Regardless, when people are not functioning at their best, the program will suffer.

While all of the contributors to an instruction program should feel invested in its success and ongoing development, the Instruction Coordinator is typically the individual charged with responsibility for monitoring the program and addressing concerns or problems that arise. This entire process, from taking stock to assessment to correcting course, is part of a loop in which an Instruction Coordinator continuously analyzes the program, the library, and the institution to ensure that all are in alignment. This chapter provides examples of some of the common setbacks faced by academic library instruction programs, along with recommendations for diagnosing these issues, identifying their root causes, and leading the program and the organization through the difficult process of getting back on course.

THE FOUR FRAMES AND ACADEMIC LEADERSHIP

When a program goes astray, an Instruction Coordinator may need to look more closely at the nested rings of their organization: the teaching librarians within the instruction group, the instruction group within the library, and the library within the institution. Some issues are not specific to the instruction program itself, but express underlying tensions within an organization or the wider institutional culture.

One strategy for understanding and making adjustments within an organization is the Four-Frame Model, as developed by Bolman and Deal in their 1991 book, *Reframing Organizations: Artistry, Choice, and Leadership*. In this model, the four frames reflect perspectives through which one can understand an organization. The challenge this model presents is how to incorporate views from all four frames, whether in managing the organization, making decisions, dealing with conflict, or planning long-term strategy (Sowell, 2014, p. 216). Bolman and Deal's (1991) four frames are:

- **Structural**, which relates to goals, responsibilities, roles, and systems;
- **Human Resource**, which is tied to skills, needs, feelings, and interactions between individuals and the organization;
- **Political**, which pertains to power, access to resources, and competing interests; and
- **Symbolic**, which incorporates to culture and the "story" of the organization.

As Giesecke (2007) notes, three of the four frames (Human Resource, Political, Symbolic) relate to emotionally intelligent leadership. These three frames involve understanding the emotions of others, understanding one's own emotions to interact effectively and build relationships, and interpreting events with an awareness of those events' emotional and affective dimensions (Giesecke, 2007, pp. 76–77).

The four frames have been applied in a variety of organizational settings, and the model's implications for academic leaders are fully explored in *Reframing Academic Leadership* (Bolman & Gallos, 2011), which is the core text in the Harvard Leadership Institute for Academic Librarians (LIAL), an annual weeklong course attended by many academic library managers and leaders. Perhaps in part because of the model's exploration at LIAL, there are several examples of its use in the context of libraries and librarianship.

Head and Brown (1995) state that the rapid pace of change in libraries necessitates engagement with "concepts from organizational theory and discoveries about effective management and leadership practices"; they present the four frames as a tool for approaching the increasing complexity of the library as an organization (p. 1). Sowell (2014) views the reorganization of an academic library's collection management department through the four frames and asserts that a "multi-frame perspective [can] help an academic library continue to evolve the paradigm" for its programs and services (p. 212). Even the perpetual questions of how librarians are perceived in academia and of what role tenure (or the lack thereof) plays in this dynamic have been considered through the four frames. Fleming-May and Douglass (2014) employ the frames to gather new insights about the place of librarians in the academy and propose how librarians' strategic efforts in the political and symbolic frames have the potential to "increase [librarians'] esteem in the eyes of disciplinary faculty" (p. 405).

An instruction program can also be seen through each of the four organizational frames. In the Structural frame is the program itself: the understanding of its components, the roles for participants in the program, and its intended outcomes. The Human Resource frame includes the individuals who teach and the instruction unit or team. The library and campus stakeholders are situated within the perspective of the Political frame, as well as the connections and collaborations that create the foundation of the program. Finally, the Symbolic frame is the story the Coordinator tells about the program to engage participants, students, and other stakeholders; the essence of why an academic library instruction program is valuable and an essential contributor to teaching and learning.

Individual leaders are often strongest in one or two frames, not all four, which means that the natural inclination is to view an organization through these preferred frames without taking in the full picture. Therefore, when diagnosing and addressing a problem within an organization, a leader may focus their efforts on what is most comfortable and familiar to them, which can cause a mismatch between problems and solutions while impeding organizational growth. As Head and Brown (1995) explain:

> The single frame, no matter how unique, is usually derived from the manager's personalized view of management concepts and/or from direct experiences. This style of analysis stems from the manager's need for uniformity, predictability, and stability; perceived ingredients of managerial success. The danger with the single frame approach is that it constrains the manager to act in a certain, predisposed manner. This managerial action is often dependent on past experience and assumptions, which may be relevant to the problem at hand, or not. (p. 5)

However, Bolman and Gallos (2011) propose that "academic leaders are skilled in the art of *reframing*—a deliberate process of shifting perspectives to see the same situation in multiple ways and through different lenses" (p. 13). Reframing is a reflective practice that entails soliciting input from others, embracing growth opportunities, anticipating the future, and "breaking frame" to push beyond what is known and comfortable (Bolman & Gallos, 2011, p. 25). These skills are essential for an Instruction Coordinator as they develop an instruction program, monitor the health of the program, situate the program within its organization and institution, and change direction if necessary.

ASKING DIFFICULT QUESTIONS

Unfortunately, it is impossible to prevent an instruction program from *ever* encountering *any* setbacks. However, an intentional Instruction Coordinator who asks difficult questions about the program and where it is going is better equipped to respond to the challenges that arise and even to identify potential issues before they push an instruction program off course. As Bolman and Gallos (2011) note, "learning to make deep, accurate, and quick situational diagnoses requires slowing down"—even though this might feel counterintuitive in a too-busy workday (p. 24).

Table 8.1. Asking Difficult Questions About an Instruction Program

What do the numbers say?	**Analyze** Review the longitudinal statistics for the instruction program and identify trends and outliers. **Reflect** • Are there any changes—or noticeable plateaus—in the number of sessions offered or the number of attendees? • Do you recognize any demographic shifts (e.g., fewer undergraduates in literature review workshops; more graduate students in citation management workshops; particular academic departments that seem over- or under-represented in the instruction program)? • Do the numbers correspond with institutional enrollment trends?
What do the students say?	**Analyze** Review evaluations or other assessment data. **Reflect** • Are there any changes or emerging trends in the feedback provided by students, or in post-session assessments designed to measure or capture what students have learned? **Analyze** If possible, review evaluations and assessment instruments alongside the stated learning objectives and lesson plan for an instruction session. **Reflect** • Were the objectives met? How did students respond to the teaching librarian's content, method of delivery,

What do the faculty say?

and pedagogical approaches? Did the session align with students' expectations?

Analyze
Ask teaching librarians to review their email correspondence with faculty regarding library instruction.
Reflect
- If a faculty member declines the offer of an instruction session for a course, do they provide a reason (e.g., lack of time, lack of relevance to the course)?
- Or, if a faculty member has requested instruction sessions in the past but now declines, have they indicated why?

Analyze
Review any other feedback from faculty about library instruction—written evaluations, emails sent after a session, notes or quotes from conversations.
Reflect
- What does this feedback tell you about the faculty member's experience (neutral, positive, or negative) with library instruction?

What do the teaching librarians say?

Analyze
Review teaching evaluations and/or conduct focus groups or interviews with librarians in the instruction program.
Reflect
- What works well about the instruction program?
- What, if anything, would they change?
- Does the program have a clear purpose/mission that continues to resonate for those who teach in it?

- Do librarians have the resources and infrastructure they need (e.g., adequate time, professional development opportunities, appropriate teaching spaces) to contribute effectively to the program?
- Are roles and expectations for *individual* teaching librarians, and for the *team* of teaching librarians, clearly defined?

The prompts in Table 8.1 can guide Instruction Coordinators in reflection and thoughtful consideration, to diagnose what ails an instruction program. In addition to gathering and analyzing data related to the instruction program, several reflective questions for diagnosis are presented. A Coordinator might ask teaching librarians to reflect on some or all of these questions and share their responses. According to Head and Brown (1995), "reframing techniques should not be the restricted tools of managers," because "staff affected by change" can provide additional insight and valuable perspectives (p. 6). Coordinators can consider using these prompts as discussion topics at an annual instruction retreat, or as part of the departmental or personal goal-setting process, but these prompts should absolutely not be used as fodder for weekly self-criticism sessions. The intention is to look at the program over the longer term, and within the wider contexts of the library organization and the institution in which it is situated, without changing direction from day to day in response to the slightest shift.

With this feedback, one might apply the Four-Frame Model, as outlined in the following; conduct a SWOT Analysis, a model commonly used in business environments and in strategic planning processes to assess a program's strengths, weaknesses, opportunities, and threats; or engage in a card sort exercise with a group of teaching librarians to set priorities for improving specific features of the program. Card sorting is an organizational diagnostic method often found in usability studies and is a good way of gathering feedback and direction from users (in this case, the teaching librarians). Creative problem-solving methods as proposed by Grassian and Kaplowitz (2005, pp. 74–83) can also be used to engage an instruction team. Regardless of which approach or set of approaches a Coordinator takes, they should ask many questions and take time to review and synthesize the answers with an open mind. The method of engagement is secondary to the process of reflection and the experience of considering an instruction program from a variety of perspectives.

Bear in mind, however, that this may not be an easy exercise to undertake, whether it is done by the Coordinator or by the entire instruction team. Diagnosis and reflection require vulnerability and may cause discomfort either for individuals or for the group. For more discussion on having these conversations, see "Psychological Safety and Difficult Conversations" in Textbox 8.1.

Textbox 8.1. Psychological Safety and Difficult Conversations

CONTRIBUTED BY MELANIE MAKSIN

In her book *Dare to Lead*, Brene Brown (2018) asserts that "[o]ur ability to be daring leaders will never be greater than our capacity for vulnerability" (p. 11). Vulnerability is neither a weakness nor a fatal flaw; instead, it is the ability to reflect honestly, interact authentically, and take responsibility. Vulnerability, not to be confused with "oversharing," brings intentionality and humanity into the workplace.

Related to the concept of vulnerability is the need to foster the conditions in which this vulnerability can be practiced without fear or shame. Edmondson (2018) emphasizes the need for *psychological safety* within a team or organization:

> Psychological safety is broadly defined as a climate in which people are comfortable expressing and being themselves. More specifically, when people have psychological safety at work, they feel comfortable sharing concerns and mistakes without fear of embarrassment or retribution. They are confident that they can speak up and won't be humiliated, ignored, or blamed. They know they can ask questions when they are unsure about something. They tend to trust and respect their colleagues. (p. xvi)

Both Edmondson (2018) and Brown (2018) point to the findings of Google's Project Aristotle, which studied high-functioning teams and discovered that the "most important" dynamic within a team is "psychological safety—team members feeling safe to take risks and be vulnerable in front of each other" (Brown, 2018, p. 36).

The concepts of vulnerability and psychological safety may be worth considering before embarking on difficult conversations about an instruction program and individuals' roles in it. If colleagues are unable to share the challenges they face or speak openly about their concerns, attempts at deep discussions will remain surface-level and shallow. Strategies that Edmondson (2018) proposes to build psychology safety within a team include developing a culture of listening (p. 87) and emphasizing interdependence (p. 162), along with "speak[ing] up, ask[ing] questions, debat[ing] vigorously, and commit[ting] to continuous learning and improvement" (p. 103).

VIEWING A WAYWARD INSTRUCTION PROGRAM THROUGH (THREE OF) THE FOUR FRAMES

There are many ways to analyze and synthesize the feedback gathered on the state of an instruction program. This section outlines three of the four frames and recommends strategies for addressing common program setbacks through a multiframe approach. The Human Resource frame is considered in its section, due to its fairly complex nature.

The Structural Frame

Bolman and Deal's (1991) Structural frame is concerned with responsibilities, resources, policies, procedures, and goals. It "emphasizes an organization's design and the formal roles and relationships of individuals within the organization" (Benjes-Small & Miller, 2017, p. 47). To regard an instruction program through the Structural frame is to examine the architecture of the program, the nuts and bolts that hold it together, and the various organizational charts (within and outside of the library) that map formal relationships across departments and groups.

Structural challenges may be seen in:

- Low attendance in workshops
- Lack of integration into the curriculum
- Student evaluations that suggest that learning objectives have not been met
- Expansion of the program without appropriate adjustments for scale

To contend with these and other structural issues, an Instruction Coordinator may consider the view through the Political frame, and nurture strategic partnerships with faculty, departments, and administrators inside and outside the library. For example, instruction librarians and their faculty allies can work together to better align course-integrated instruction and workshops with students' needs, and these allies can help their students understand how the library's offerings complement and enrich classroom learning. Similarly, if the size and scope of an instruction program have snowballed and instruction librarians are unable to keep up with demand, an Instruction Coordinator can use their political acumen to make the case to library administrators that the instruction program needs increased resources.

The Political Frame

The Political frame encompasses competition for resources, the development of strategic alliances and partnerships, and awareness of the varied interests of stakeholders. Although librarians rarely think of themselves as political actors, most Instruction Coordinators are aware of the political pressures on an instruction program. For example, how do faculty regard teaching librarians, and what impact does this have on the ability of librarians to contribute to teaching and learning initiatives? Is library administration willing to prioritize the instruction program and provide it with the resources it needs to grow and thrive? Other political issues may include:

- Diminished interest from faculty who request "the same thing as last year" or perceive library instruction as "sacrificing" class time
- Lack of collaboration with key partners on campus, including writing centers and teaching and learning centers
- Lack of meaningful support for the program from library administrators

A Coordinator might pivot from the Political frame to the Symbolic frame to address these and similar issues. Advocacy efforts (as discussed in Chapter 6) and the results of assessment (more about this in Chapter 7) often derive meaning from the stories that develop out of the importance and impact of librarians' work. For example, if the library seeks to build a partnership with the campus writing center to provide deeper support for students throughout the entire research and writing process, the Instruction Coordinator can tailor their outreach to the writing center by focusing on the shared values and common approaches of the two organizations. In a politically charged environment, the library and the writing center might be understood as "competitors" for resources from the institution; with symbolic reframing, however, the two groups can become allies in providing comprehensive, cross-disciplinary support to students.

The Symbolic Frame

The Symbolic frame "emphasizes meaning and belief" (Benjes-Small & Miller, 2017, p. 49). This frame is connected to an organization's culture and values, how those values are experienced and lived within the organization, and the stories that the organization tells for internal or external consumption. An instruction program may have its own culture, values, and story within the larger library's culture, values, and story; and those are each further connected to the institution's culture, values, and story.

Ideally, these meanings and beliefs will be harmonious. When cacophony occurs, the Symbolic frame may reveal underlying issues, including:

- Misalignment of the program's components with the program's mission/vision/goals

- Misalignment of the instruction program with the library's overall mission/vision/goals
- Misalignment of the instruction program with the institution's culture of teaching and learning and stated needs

These issues (i.e., is the instruction program relevant, resonant, and appropriately aligned with its library and institution?) can benefit from structural reframing. To accomplish this, an Instruction Coordinator can return to the landscape they uncovered when taking stock. Perhaps elements of the landscape have changed or shifted; new administrators, new programs, or new pressures can all cause unbalance in the library's teaching and learning efforts. Even the instruction program's internal landscape, including its contributors and resources, may have changed significantly enough to alter the program's course. This is a prime opportunity to reach out once again to participants and other stakeholders to engage them in discussion and revision of the instruction program as a whole.

THE VIEW FROM THE FOURTH FRAME: OR, WHEN PEOPLE AND TEAMS GO ASTRAY

Although each of the four frames reflects the inherent complexity of any organization, the Human Resource frame can seem especially complicated and its issues particularly thorny. All instruction programs, regardless of how many teaching librarians contribute and how it is supervised and led, consist of people. The Human Resource frame considers how individuals participate in the program, how they relate to their colleagues, how they relate to the Instruction Coordinator, and how an instruction team, whether it consists of two, 10, or 20 teaching librarians, functions.

Some common issues in the Human Resource frame include burnout in individuals, interpersonal conflict, and dysfunction in teams, all of which can impact the effectiveness and long-term success of an instruction program. These challenges are not exclusive to academic library instruction programs, of course, but there may be factors related to the work of teaching, and to the instruction program and its place in the library and the institution, that bring these issues to the forefront.

Burnout

Maslach and Jackson (1981) define burnout as "a syndrome of emotional exhaustion and cynicism that occurs among individuals who do 'people-work' of some kind" (p. 99). Burnout can have a serious impact on the emotional, physical, and social health of an employee, can contribute to job turnover, and leads to lower quality of service in the workplace (Maslach &

Jackson, 1981). Librarians and others in "helping professions" can be more susceptible to burnout; academic teaching librarians, in particular, might experience burnout due to the demands of their jobs, the sometimes unpredictable and long hours during the height of the "teaching season," and the expectations placed on them by colleagues. Instruction Coordinators may also suffer from burnout, which is discussed in more detail in the following chapter.

Affleck (1996), Becker (1993), and Patterson and Howell (1990) found that the telltale characteristics of burnout—emotional exhaustion, depersonalization, and a diminished sense of personal accomplishment—were present among many of the instruction librarians they surveyed. Sheesley (2001) identifies a variety of possible causes of burnout in instruction librarians, including repetitive work (i.e., teaching multiple sections of the same class), inadequate staffing or resources, lack of teaching experience and inability to meet instruction program expectations, and lack of positive feedback or recognition for their instruction work (p. 448). Burnout may manifest in a librarian's low engagement with the instruction program or a reliance on repetitive teaching, but the *causes* of burnout may stem from challenges within the organization, not an individual librarian's stress level or behaviors (Sheesley, 2001). With this in mind, an Instruction Coordinator might coach a burned-out instruction librarian to identify professional development opportunities or pursue other strategies for reengaging with the work, while also exploring possible structural adjustments to the instruction program, including clarifying programmatic goals, examining the allocation of resources, and developing improved training and feedback mechanisms for all teaching librarians.

INTERPERSONAL CONFLICT, GROUP DYSFUNCTION, AND CULTURE CLASHES

Although the size and composition of an instruction group will vary, interpersonal challenges are just as likely to arise within the smallest teams as they are among the most sprawling network of contributors. Instruction librarians may increasingly be expected to collaborate and co-teach with colleagues whose teaching styles do not mesh with their own. Librarians with liaison roles or subject area expertise may feel that they are competing against functional experts (e.g., digital humanists or research data management librarians) for instruction opportunities, particularly as these functional roles assume greater relevance and visibility in academic libraries.

Instruction librarians and their Coordinator can also find themselves at odds. The Coordinator is in the position of encouraging autonomy and creativity while still maintaining focus on the instruction program's goals. This relationship can be further complicated when the Instruction Coordinator does not directly supervise the instruction librarians and is tasked with getting buy-in and creating a team among the librarians who teach.

Academic libraries are not immune to workplace dysfunction. Freedman and Vreven (2017) explore the extremes of dysfunction in their study of bullying in academic libraries, finding that incivility, hostility, harassment, and intimidation are among the many measures of bullying present in these workplaces (p. 734). The "enabling structures" of bullying among academic library staff, as identified by Freedman and Vreven (2016), include:

> *tension between librarians and teaching faculty and/or administration, the changing and often marginalized role of librarians in the learning and teaching processes,* demands and pressures of providing library services ubiquitously in a digital environment, and the academic library culture that may adapt quickly or not. (p. 731, emphasis added)

Within this pressure cooker, bullying is just one type of negative experience that can lead to low morale. According to Kendrick (2017), low morale in academic libraries is typically triggered by an unexpected event that then turns into a longer cycle of abuse.

Unease is also often present concerning instruction librarians' identity as a teacher. While Chapter 3 discussed how to foster this identity (through CoPs, peer-teaching observation programs, etc.), it is worth noting that there are several factors related to professional drive or purpose that can negatively contribute to interpersonal conflict within a library organization. Instruction librarians may find that their colleagues question the teaching role of librarians and "have conflicting attitudes about the appropriate role of public service, that is, whether the librarian's mission is to provide information or teach library users how to find information" (Sheesley, 2001, p. 448). Misconceptions or misunderstandings related to the role of the library in advancing teaching and learning can create stress for individual teaching librarians, perhaps resulting in imposter syndrome (Clark, Vardeman, & Barba, 2014; Martinez & Forrey, 2019; Parkman, 2016), and can negatively affect the instruction programs' success.

Conflict in an instruction program can come from many different areas, including communication issues, ineffective collaboration (which may be attributed to culture, attitudes, trust, or distance), resistance to change, and role conflict and morale among the instruction team. Depending on organizational dynamics, there may also exist a conflict or dysfunction between teaching librarians and the rest of the library; this can be attributed, in some institutions, to the fact that the teaching librarians are often considered the "face" of the library. The Instruction Coordinator must constantly and systematically take the pulse of the program and their instruction librarians, managing changes and making adjustments as necessary.

EMBRACING FAILURE... AND MOVING ON

It is extremely rare that every aspect of a program, especially a complex teaching and learning program, will be absolutely perfect—and the elements of the program that are successful at one time or in a particular context are unlikely to remain successful if left on autopilot. The maintenance of an instruction program is like lesson planning and teaching: iterative and improved by reflection and assessment (Benjes-Small & Miller, 2017). A program that has gone astray can be redeemed through thoughtful, intentional adjustments.

Although the leadership and management literature underscores the role of the leader/manager/supervisor in steering programmatic efforts and supporting individuals and teams, this does not mean that transforming an entire workplace culture, or singlehandedly solving everyone's problems, is the purview of any one person within the organization. The responsibility for the entire instruction team's interpersonal concerns, productivity issues, and interactions with its broader organizational culture cannot, and should not, rest solely on the shoulders of the Instruction Coordinator. The chapter that follows proposes ways in which an Instruction Coordinator can continually grow in their leadership praxis while remaining aware of the pressures and pitfalls that can lead to burnout.

When managing the common (or uncommon) challenges that face an instruction program, the most important thing is for a Coordinator to remain flexible, strategic, and intentional in dealing with the issues that arise. Even an aspect of a program that seems like a "failure" is an opportunity for growth.

Chapter Nine

Growing as an Instruction Coordinator

BACK TO WHERE IT ALL BEGAN

With the final chapter of this book, it is important to circle back around to the leader of the instruction program. Once again, this leader could be someone with the official title of Instruction Coordinator, someone who is unofficially in charge of library instruction efforts, an administrator that oversees the library's teaching and learning program, or even a solo librarian that handles all of their library's instructional efforts along with basic library operations. While the majority of this book has focused on managing or directing the instruction program itself, it should be acknowledged that a program is only as successful as the librarian(s) leading it. Chapter 3 introduced the idea of CoPs for librarians in teaching and learning programs; as discussed, an Instruction Coordinator needs to facilitate skill development and a sense of community among the research and instruction librarians they coordinate and work alongside. Unsurprisingly (particularly for those that are leading instruction programs already), it is also extremely important for the Coordinator to take steps to cultivate their personal and professional growth and development. This chapter discusses strategies and techniques for Instruction Coordinators to focus on their development, which is an essential practice if they want to perform their best as intentional and authentic leaders.

BURNOUT FOR THE INSTRUCTION COORDINATOR

The previous chapter examined burnout in teaching librarians; however, burnout is also an issue for Instruction Coordinators. A wide variety of factors can contribute to burnout in Coordinators, many of which have already been touched on. It must be acknowledged, however, that the work discussed in this book is both laboriously and emotionally taxing; Arellano Douglas and Gadsby (2019) note that, "the skills and labor involved in library instruction Coordinator work—developing pedagogical training, coordinating information literacy (IL) curricular integration and assessment, and training teaching librarians—includes an intense investment in the quality of relationships with others" (para 1). Arellano Douglas and Gadsby (2019) discuss this phenomenon within the framework of Fletcher's (1998) categories of relational practice, identifying issues that affect Instruction Coordinators, including emotional strategizing (e.g., maintaining "relational awareness to build and sustain connections advantageous to advancing the instruction program"); preserving (e.g., taking on administrative tasks and/or the "work that no one wants to do"); mutual empowering (e.g., building expertise in colleagues); creating teams (e.g., facilitating information sharing and collaboration); and workload and staffing challenges. This last factor, in particular, touches on the often selfless, or perhaps more accurately *overburdened*, nature of library work in general. The application to Coordinator roles is fairly striking:

> The work of liaising with faculty, teaching, and reference is the work of an instruction librarian, but many of the instruction coordinators we interviewed did that work *as well as* the work of building and sustaining both an instruction team and an instruction program. (Arellano Douglas & Gadsby, 2019, para. 33)

Instruction Coordinators are often put in the near-impossible position of leading teaching and learning programs while also performing a range of additional responsibilities. While this does have benefits, in that it allows the Coordinator to stay connected to the classroom in ways that more senior administrators often miss out on, it can also cause undue burden by increasing the responsibilities of the person in this position, throwing off any balance they may have already achieved in their role. The mere act of being a leader can be exceedingly challenging, and the challenges are often compounded by the nature of the work of coordinating both people and a program.

Servant Leadership

Many librarians at the helm of instruction programs may be categorized or identify as servant leaders. Servant leadership is characterized by a leader that shares power, puts the needs and priorities of others first, and helps their team develop and perform at their best (Greenleaf, 1977). The dimensions often associated with servant leadership may seem quite similar to the dispositions reflected on in Chapter 1; Spears (1998) mentions characteristics including listening, empathy, healing, awareness, persuasion, conceptualization, foresight, stewardship, commitment, and community building. On the one hand, fostering and strengthening these dispositions and skill sets is an important part of one's growth and development. However, the benefits of this growth may take time to develop, and in the meantime, the focus on others' needs may end up being a detriment.

As previously discussed, burnout can afflict all instruction librarians—but it is important to spend some time looking at the impact of burnout specifically on Instruction Coordinators. Arellano Douglas and Gadsby (2017) note that expectations often contributing to burnout are particularly more nuanced for female Instruction Coordinators, arguing that:

> instruction coordinator job responsibilities are primarily relational activity coded as feminine labor, and that this job role is subject to many of the gendered expectations associated with women. This intersection of workplace structures and gender bias results in the undervaluing of instruction coordinator work, which negatively affects potential career advancement opportunities for women in academic libraries. (p. 266)

According to Arellano Douglas and Gadsby (2017), expected behaviors for female employees, including mentoring, coaching, and supporting, are invisible behaviors that are taken on by Instruction Coordinators (who, according to their research, are predominantly female). These characteristics are similar to those of servant leadership, and a Coordinator needs to recognize and acknowledge these issues (see Textbox 9.1) to move forward and grow in their role or, conversely, identify when it might be time to move on or make a change.

Textbox 9.1. Put It in Practice: Identifying Burnout

Answering these questions can help you recognize burnout. On a scale of 1 (never) to 10 (frequently), how often do you:

- Feel emotionally drained from your work?
- Feel frustrated by your job?
- Lose interest in things you once were passionate about?
- Feel you have accomplished worthwhile things in your job?
- Have a lack of caring toward colleagues?
- Feel fatigued when you get up in the morning?

Source: Adapted from Maslach and Jackson (1981)

Sacrifice Syndrome

Another consideration that can increase feelings of burnout is Sacrifice Syndrome, which is "a vicious circle leading to mental and physical distress" that is caused by long-term exposure to vocational and leadership stressors (McKee, Johnston, & Massimilian, 2006, p. 1). Alire (2007) discusses the negative effects of Sacrifice Syndrome:

> The syndrome renders leaders totally ineffective because they are so busy with *giving* all the time and striving for excellence that they begin ignoring their own personal and professional well-being. Leaders then find themselves in a negative spiral starting with unhappiness and anxiety and leading to meaningless actions, which then causes chronic stress. (p. 98)

Awareness of factors such as the high expectations of leaders, the possibility of Sacrifice Syndrome, and the signs of burnout is crucial for Instruction Coordinators, and should be part of their consistent regime of self-care and growth (more on how this can be worked into one's regular routine is addressed shortly). If, as Arellano Douglas and Gadsby (2017) argue, female Instruction Coordinators are more apt to succumb to gendered expectations, then they may be at a greater danger of succumbing to burnout syndrome. The next section discusses strategies for moving past burnout.

Avoiding Burnout

While it may seem counterintuitive to distance oneself from the librarians with which an Instruction Coordinator is trying to build community and create trust, creating a bit of distance is necessary to maintain perspective:

> caring professionals who serve individuals in need require simultaneous openness to and distance from those they seek to aid. They need clear boundaries to sustain objectivity, protect themselves from the stress of the work, and nurture autonomy in others. At the same time [. . .] good academic leaders need to understand others at a deep level in order to respond in appropriate ways to the unique realities of situations over time. (Bolman & Gallos, 2011, pp. 189–190)

Creating boundaries between a leader and those they lead is necessary for creating a balance that allows the leader to approach problems or issues with a clear head. Personal boundaries for leaders are also important for maintaining well-being; one strategy for overcoming the blurring of the personal and the professional, suggested by Bolman and Gallos (2011), is that academic leaders be wary of taking on too much themselves and thus not challenging others, which is a "road to burnout and failure" (p. 194).

For many Instruction Coordinators (especially solo librarians coordinating "programs of one"), it is easy to get bogged down by the administrative details and priorities of running an instruction program. This often leaves little time for the Coordinator to focus on themselves and their teaching practice. Focusing inward is often a struggle in a job that is filled with external demands on one's time and resources; however, this act is essential for recognizing and moving on from burnout. Finding ways to renew individual passions and pedagogical interests can help alleviate feelings of burnout. This renewal might manifest itself as trying a new activity during a course-related instruction session, teaching a new workshop topic, or having a chat with a colleague. Being intentional about the Coordinator's own development and growth is extremely important for both recovering from and avoiding burnout in the future.

GROWTH AND RENEWAL

So, how does one begin to focus on the renewal of their practice? Identifying the key characteristics for Instruction Coordinators, as described in Chapter 1, is one way to help center the work of the Coordinator. For example, the trait of *intentionality* has been mentioned, not only for the instruction program, but also for an individual's development and purpose. Asking reflective questions about these characteristics can help with recentering and reflecting on areas where the Coordinator feels development is necessary. Chow and Rich (2013) found the following qualities to be most ideal in library leaders: empathy, vision, communication, flexibility, delegation, and integrity; empathy and integrity, in particular, are desired in almost all types of library administrators. This certainly has implications for Instruction Coordinators, since, as seen in the earlier discussion, these qualities often lead to feelings of overburdening and burnout. As a result, Coordinators must focus on their growth and renewal; this can also be useful in counteracting burnout and lack of job engagement, which can afflict any professionals, but particularly those in leadership roles.

In a study of close to 300 employees in a high-tech company, Caniëls et al. (2018) found a direct link between proactive personalities and job engagement, indicating that employees in an organization, including leaders, with a "growth mindset" benefit from the opportunity to cultivate their growth (p. 61), which results in more job satisfaction and engagement. Ideally, upper administration should make room for this type of work with library middle managers and anyone in a leadership role, but it may indeed be necessary for the leader to take on this type of reflective practice on their own.

Whether or not Coordinators have support or encouragement from their supervisors in moving past (or even better, avoiding) burnout, there are methods for engaging in this work individually. McKee, Johnston, and Massimilian (2006) suggest three crucial components for leaders to sustain their work and experience renewal: mindfulness, hope, and compassion. In particular, mindfulness exercises are a positive way to combat burnout and Sacrifice Syndrome; for example, reflecting internally on questions such as:

- Is my work meeting my professional goals and passions?
- Am I achieving (personally or professionally) what I have set out to accomplish?
- Am I connecting with friends/family/colleagues in a way that feels authentic and intentional?

Building in "consistent practice of this discipline establishes trust and helps create an environment in which you get proactive feedback, nurture authentic relationships and foster reliable followers" (McKee, Johnston, & Massimilian, 2006, p. 3). The three elements suggested by McKee, Johnston, and Massimilian (2006) contribute to sustainability and help leaders "manage their strengths" (Alire, 2007, p. 99) over time.

Personal Development

There are many techniques for developing intentionally as a leader/director/Coordinator, or any other organizational configuration one might find themselves in. Likewise, the idea of *personal development* can certainly mean different things for different people. No matter what, steps taken in this area should help with recentering oneself and contributing to growth and renewal efforts; above all, these steps should be intentional and authentic. As Arellano Douglas (2019) comments,

> Part of reshaping the structures that influence our teaching involves centering what we value and making that our focus. It involves asking ourselves what we really care about, because once we figure that out we can bend walls to support us and our work rather than impede it. (para. 39)

Leadership Development

For those leading a team of instruction librarians (whether in a supervisory capacity or otherwise), it can also be a useful exercise to engage in reflection of one's leadership style with the teaching team or other stakeholders. Have stakeholders noticed a change in the Coordinator's focus or behavior? Often, burnout is recognizable to others before it is to the individual experiencing it. Engaging colleagues in a leadership self-assessment, such as the 360-degree assessment (Maxwell, 2005) can provide a much-needed recentering. The 360 method is particularly useful for Coordinators since they often fall solidly within the definition of "middle management." As Maxwell (2005) reflects,

> If you are a leader in the middle of an organization, you don't need me to tell you that you have a challenging job. Many of the middle leaders I meet are frustrated, tense, and sometimes tempted to quit. I hear them say things such as, "It's like banging my head against a brick wall." "No matter how hard I try, I never seem to get anywhere." "I really wonder if it's all worth it." (p. 23)

These statements are likely quite familiar for many Coordinators. Having colleagues within the organization that are above, beside, and below the Coordinator complete a 360 assessment, or other similar leadership evaluation, will help the Coordinator see their strengths and weaknesses in terms of skills and influence, allowing them to reengage their development in certain areas to be the most effective leader they can.

Personal Strategic Planning

While Instruction Coordinators are likely intimately familiar with the process of strategic planning, they often engage in this work with their instruction programs, the larger library organization, or their institution. However, strategic planning can also serve as a useful method by which Coordinators can refocus their energies and align their personal and professional values. A Personal Strategic Plan (PSP) is:

> a disciplined thought process that produces fundamental decisions and actions that shape and guide who you are, where you are going, what you do and how, when and why you do it [and] is done with a focus on the future. (Garcia, 2016, p. 38)

PSPs can be informal or formal, but should be developed by the individual rather than their organization. For more formalized PSPs, Duffus (2004) recommends the following elements: a resume; a personal analysis, including objectives, strengths and weaknesses; a background analysis, listing connections with the individual's organization; "strategies to achieve short term and strategic objectives"; an action plan to achieve objectives; and an assessment plan (pp. 146–47). Hinojosa (2012) cautions against looking far ahead to desired outcomes: "future scenarios may be useful for reflection, yet they may not help us create our own personal strategic plans because they are based on events that are plausible but may not be grounded in our personal circumstances" (p. 35). Focusing on a shorter time frame for personal development can help prevent unforeseen obstacles.

A PSP should also incorporate a personal vision, mission, and guiding principles; articulating these statements will help Coordinators align their life goals with their professional goals (more on this next). This is also an area in which library administrators can foster personal development of their staff; Lo and Herman (2017) found that "library employees highly value living consistently with their values and beliefs" and employees that can participate in personal visioning report a higher level of mental well-being and are more likely to engage in creative and intellectual pursuits (p. 803).

Professional Development

A renewed interest could also take the form of reengaging with one's professional network and passions; this could mean focusing on strengthening professional connections or exploring new opportunities to facilitate learning and professional growth.

Personal Learning Networks

Personal Learning Networks, or PLNs, "are a reciprocal learning system in which educators participate by sharing with and learning from others" (Nussbaum-Beach, 2012/2013, p. 26). PLNs have a far-reaching effect on professional growth and development because, as Nussbaum-Beach (2012/2013) remarks, they "help boost your energy, stimulate personal growth, and lead to a revitalized individual" (p. 26). The makeup of PLNs can come from many sources. Developing a digital PLN is especially useful for Instruction Coordinators that do not have peers in their organization doing the same work, or solo librarians that do both the teaching and coordinating of an instruction program. Using social media or other types of online communities (e.g., listservs), Coordinators can develop a network of support that is not constrained by geographic location or size of their library:

> PLNs consist of a learner and the contacts and colleagues with whom they surround themselves. These networks need not occur face-to-face or in real time, nor does the learner have to personally know their knowledge collaborators. PLNs are often specifically devoted to professional learning and development, and are keenly applicable to the use technology [sic], which makes them as local or global in reach as the learner desires. (Cooke, 2012, p. 7)

By engaging in connected digital networks, Instruction Coordinators will have easy access to colleagues to use as sounding boards and potential future collaborators.

According to Elliott (2009), two crucial factors to maintaining a successful and advantageous PLN are ownership and commitment. Coordinators should examine what they hope to get out of their PLN, and how much time they can and are willing to invest:

> You are the centre of your learning network. You speak in your own voice and can share ideas and opinions in which you believe. It's also an opportunity for self-directed learning; your interests, in your time, at your level of involvement. (Elliott, 2009, p. 49)

Perhaps one potential goal of a PLN for Instruction Coordinators might be to develop relationships with colleagues to discuss teaching and learning on a broader scale. This could easily evolve into collaborative SoTL projects or conference presentations, activities that provide professional growth but also allow the Coordinator to explore teaching and learning outside of their institution.

Conferences and Workshops

The profession of academic librarianship has many rewarding and content-rich conferences devoted to information literacy instruction (Textbox 9.2). These conferences are an excellent option to not only share one's research and professional successes but also for gaining perspectives to other institutional contexts, as well as grow PLNs and learn from the successes and failures of peers. Mata, Lathame, and Ransome (2010) see professional involvement as an evolutionary process: "first, one joins and then begins attending and presenting at conferences. This participation can facilitate networking, skill-building, collaboration, and mentoring. Consequently, conferences may contribute to increased professional development, collaboration, and advocacy" (p. 453). Tomaszewski and MacDonald (2009) touch on the importance of attending subject-specific conferences, particularly for those librarians with liaison appointments. This practice can also be useful for those coordinating liaison programs by providing the Coordinator with an overview of multidisciplinary trends and curricular advancements.

Textbox 9.2. Selected Library Instruction Conferences

- Association of College and Research Libraries (ACRL), http://www.ala.org/acrl/conferences. Note: Many state or regional ACRL groups have conferences as well; some, including ACRL New England, offer training and conferences specifically related to instruction.
- European Conference on Information Literacy (ECIL), http://ilconf.org/
- Georgia International Conference on Information Literacy, https://academics.georgiasouthern.edu/ce/conferences/infolit/
- Innovative Library Classroom, http://theinnovativelibraryclassroom.weebly.com/
- Librarians' Information Literacy Annual Conference (LILAC), https://www.lilacconference.com/WP
- Library Instruction West, https://libraryinstructionwest.weebly.com/
- LOEX, http://www.loex.org/

- Workshop for Instruction in Library Use (WILU), https://ir.lib.uwo.ca/wilu/

Due to their overarching role in teaching and learning on a campus-wide scale, Instruction Coordinators will also benefit from staying current in trends across higher education. Sometimes it is necessary to pursue professional development opportunities outside of one's disciplinary context; fortunately for Instruction Coordinators, many higher education-focused teaching and learning conferences can provide this much-needed perspective beyond the walls of library science. Textbox 9.3 provides a selected list of nonlibrary-focused teaching and learning conferences.

Textbox 9.3. Selected Higher Education and Leadership Conferences

- American Association for Adult and Continuing Education (AAACE), https://www.aaace.org/
- Association for the Study of Higher Education (ASHE), https://www.ashe.ws/conference
- EDUCAUSE Connect, https://events.educause.edu/
- International Society for Exploring Teaching and Learning (ISETL), http://www.isetl.org/
- International Society for the Scholarship of Teaching and Learning (ISSOTL), https://www.issotl.com/
- Professional and Organizational Development (POD) Network in Higher Education, https://podnetwork.org/events/

Tysick (2002) cites rejuvenation as one of the main benefits of attending conferences outside the field of librarianship:

> Immersing yourself in a discipline that you have a connection to, either through academic or work-related experience, is energizing. Talking to premier scholars in the field or listening to up-and-coming innovators is rejuvenating. Sometimes it is beneficial to step back from librarianship and see where the areas we support are going. (p. 78)

Attending conferences outside of librarianship can also have benefits for the rest of the instruction team. Subject librarians can attend disciplinary conferences to learn about the latest developments in scholarship and teaching in the fields they work with, while Instruction Coordinators can attend conferences more generally focused on pedagogy or the Scholarship of Teaching and Learning.

Tomaszewski and MacDonald (2009) touch on the importance of attending subject-specific conferences, particularly for those with liaison appointments. This practice can also be useful for those coordinating liaison programs by providing the Coordinator with an overview of multidisciplinary trends and curricular advancements. The same can also hold for memberships outside of the traditional library professional organizations. Bennett (2011) found:

> the value of non-library professional organization membership for librarians with subject responsibilities across a variety of disciplines and suggest that liaison librarians should be encouraged to join and participate in such organizations, for the benefit of both their libraries and the organization. (p. 49)

One additional point about conference attendance: librarians that do not have the budget or time to attend in-person conferences still have plenty of opportunities to build their PLN and grow as a professional. There are many professional development events, both in academic librarianship and higher education generally, that are available either on one's campus or through a variety of online modalities. Online conferences, Twitter chats, and webinars, for example, are excellent platforms for learning and participation does not require a travel budget. Many online conferences have the added benefit of being recorded, so instruction librarians can watch and learn together.

Finally, readers are encouraged to review the Appendix, An Instruction Coordinator's Bookshelf, of this book. It is a collection of the author's most consulted professional development resources, networks, and learning opportunities, many of which have gotten her through some complicated decision making while directing various teaching and learning programs.

FOCUSING ON THE INTENTIONAL, HOLISTIC SELF

This book has dealt primarily with the *Instruction Coordinator* or teaching and learning program director, but it is important to reiterate that the techniques and strategies discussed are useful across the board, even when one's role is not explicitly that of Coordinator. Personal and professional growth and development are crucial for all library leaders and can be as simple as keeping a journal, discussing professional challenges over coffee with a trusted colleague, or joining a book club completely outside of the university setting. Librarians can benefit from these learning communities, not only for building personal connections but also for their professional growth; as Cooke (2012) asserts, "collective intelligence can also be seen as an alternative source of educational power [and] contributes to the formation of knowledge communities" (p. 6).

While individuals are encouraged to take control of their growth and development, there should also be a call for action issued to library administrators and supervisors, particularly those that have an instruction or teaching and learning program in their portfolio. While extremely rewarding, the work of coordinating an instruction program can, and likely will, be overwhelming, isolating, and frustrating. Having administrative support to make personal and professional development a priority can go a long way to helping Instruction Coordinators avoid burnout. As Parry (2008) comments, professional development should be viewed by administrators as "a tool to enable staff to update their skills continually—essential in an environment of ongoing change" (p. 7).

Identifying strategies for focusing on the holistic self is crucial for grounding the work of Instruction Coordinators, and is important no matter the administrative level of one's position or the size of their organization. An instruction program's success is very much reliant on its leadership, a role which is complicated and constantly evolving. Miller-Young et al. (2017) eloquently and succinctly capture the complex nature of higher education leadership: "successful leadership is situational, embedded in a context that includes many individuals' narratives and skills, disciplinary cultures, types of microcultures, as well as institutional structures, communication processes, and reward systems" (p. 2). For Instruction Coordinators, intentional reflection on this definition of leadership will help guide future directions for their teaching and learning program.

Conclusion

As has been discussed throughout this book, examining instruction programs requires looking beyond just a handful of classes. Instruction program planning is a complex environment of diverse stakeholders, philosophies, approaches, and directions. Each component of the instruction program, and in hand, each measure of success, come together to create a learning environment that encourages students' growth and creativity. As the ACRL *Standards for Libraries in Higher Education* (2018) state, libraries should "partner in the educational mission of the institution to develop and support information-literate learners who can discover, access, and use information effectively for academic success, research, and lifelong learning" (p. 9). The idea of *partnership* has been a common thread throughout this book; instruction librarians partner with faculty, students, administrators, and one another. These relationships help create the foundation for an instruction program, and Instruction Coordinators must continuously nurture existing partnerships and build new ones.

Once again, it bears repeating that the techniques, questions, and directions discussed in this book can be adapted and applied to instruction programs of any context. It may require some creativity and planning to undertake a needs assessment if one finds themselves as a "program of one," but the importance of building and advocating for an instruction program is crucial for libraries of all sizes and makeups. This book concludes with a more overarching view of the challenges and opportunities facing instruction programs, as well as a glimpse into the ideal world of the academic library's place situated within their institution's teaching and learning climate.

Conclusion

CHALLENGES AND OPPORTUNITIES

For new and veteran Instruction Coordinators, there remain several continuing questions and challenges for maintaining instruction programs. Many of the challenges have been addressed throughout this book; however, it bears repeating that instruction programs require cultivation, maintenance, and advocacy to grow and succeed in their missions.

One particular set of challenges facing Instruction Coordinators is that of the expectations and requirements related to leading an instruction program. This role comes with occasional obstacles, particularly balancing responsibilities. Arellano Douglas and Gadsby (2017) urge libraries to examine and push back on the "relationally precarious position of instruction coordinators" to "shift conversations within the LIS literature from how-to's for new IL program coordinators to a more in depth questioning of what this position can and should be in the academic library" (p. 272). Instruction Coordinators must engage in a diverse range of responsibilities, including acquiring resources, managing people, and cultivating relationships, all of which can be compounded by gendered expectations. These obligations should not be shouldered by Instruction Coordinators alone, and academic library administrators have a responsibility to, as Arellano Douglas and Gadsby (2017) exhort, shift this conversation and these expectations.

An additional issue is related to resources and mission alignment. These challenges can manifest in relation to the library's internal resources (e.g., where does library instruction fit on the priority spectrum of library services? How many library staff are allocated to instruction activities? Is teaching and learning a primary component of the library's stated mission?), but can also be found externally. For example, if the university has a strong culture of teaching and learning, do campus leaders see the library as part of this culture? Alternately, if teaching and learning are not a high priority on campus, what does this mean for the library's instruction program? Many resources are necessary for library instruction programs to be successful, but this first requires full support from library administrators. It often falls to the Instruction Coordinator to secure this support. Julien, Gross, and Latham (2018) stress that "recognition and support are needed from administrators and non-librarians, and academic librarians continue to work to educate these stakeholders in the importance of information literacy and the usefulness of instructional partnerships with librarians" (p. 190). Chapters 6 and 7, which discuss advocating for and assessing an instruction program, provide strategies for accomplishing this work, but it is worth mentioning again that if administrative support—both internal and external—is not present, it can make maintaining and growing an instruction program extremely difficult.

Alongside the challenges, however, are also many opportunities. Several chapters in this book touch on issues relating to inclusivity, diversity, equity, and access to information literacy programs; the opportunities for Instruction Coordinators to incorporate these important considerations into their instruction programs are vast. Instruction Coordinators can use their instruction programs as a way to incorporate marginalized voices, both in the decision-making process (i.e., when designing information literacy curriculum) but also in terms of which library partnerships and stakeholders they collaborate with. Instruction Coordinators are in a unique position to bolster and embed conversations related to equity and diversity throughout all the library's teaching and learning efforts, thus making this work more meaningful and impactful. Tewell (2018) notes that librarians wishing to engage in and further the conversation related to equity and diversity can start by "facilitating relationships with people at one's institution who may have similar aims" as well as "seek[ing] out other librarians involved in this approach" (p. 28).

Another opportunity to consider is the shared goals in academia surrounding lifelong learning. Institutions of higher education typically hold a common pursuit of continued learning—a value that is shared by their libraries. The skills and conceptual areas of thought that underpin higher education are typically core to the mission and values of academic libraries and can also be found within the instruction program's mission statement and goals. Academic instruction librarians, in particular, are often passionate educators and are poised to positively impact the institution's teaching and learning culture by sharing these values with their colleagues on campus. This means embracing new ways of engaging with teaching and learning and taking a more active role in assessing the impact of library instruction on student learning. The push outside of the more traditional "bibliographic instruction" role is crucial to positioning librarians as leaders of teaching and learning on campus: "the librarian's role as a learned expert partnering in teaching and publishing [. . .] demonstrates the move from librarians as traditional custodians of educational materials to new roles as mentors, teachers, publishers, and content creators" (Schulte, Tiffen, Edwards, Abbott, & Luca, 2018, p. 694).

LOOKING AHEAD: A VISION FOR THE FUTURE

As readers might have intuited by this point, the author is very passionate about the role of academic librarians as partners in teaching and learning. While this book has discussed many elements that contribute to a successful library instruction program, it concludes with a call to arms, so to speak. How will librarians navigate the quickly evolving nature of higher education? What are the most critical aspects of teaching and learning that must be in place for an instruction program to succeed and thrive? In other words, a *vision for the future*.

Tearing Down Silos

For growth and success, all library instruction programs should exist hand-in-hand with teaching efforts on campus. These programs should not only contribute to student success but must be truly embedded within the culture of teaching and learning on campus. The library's instruction program is about more than isolated classroom experiences, in the way that faculty-led courses are about more than what happens in the classroom. The vision and purpose of the library's instruction program should be as lofty and as comprehensive as the most visionary academic strategic plan. Mader and Gibson (2019) urge a future that includes:

> a broader view of professional learning and faculty as learners that encompasses many stakeholders on campus. Building community from this perspective involves moving beyond the expertise found in departmental or unit-specific "silos," embracing a willingness to share and change, and welcoming everyone to contribute to larger conversations about teaching and learning. (p. 1)

In the ideal future, libraries are not just an integral part of these conversations, but serve as a catalyst for pushing conversations about teaching and learning outside of the classroom and the library to advance expectations for student learning.

Librarians as Full Partners in Teaching and Learning

Closely related to the previous mandate, for libraries to exist as an indispensable hub for teaching and learning on campus, then librarians must be treated as holistic partners in campus learning communities. In the ACRL *Roles and Strengths* document, Amsberry et al. (2017) call for a "contextual, holistic approach and wider vision which encompasses the roles and responsibilities of the instruction librarian within the academy" while recognizing that "teaching librarians have increasingly explored innovative and creative roles within their institutions" (para. 1–3). This vision is further articulated by examining the role of librarian as teaching partner:

> Being a teaching partner requires the teaching librarian to have confidence in the strengths they bring to collaborative relationships with colleagues. This expertise may include broader perspectives about information literacy, formal education in ways that information is organized and classified, expertise in research skills, and knowledge of scholarly communication models and processes. The librarian must also respect the strengths brought by the collaborator. In the best teaching partnerships, each person's contributions are valued equally. (Amsberry et al., 2017, para. 19)

Building campus relationships that position librarians as teachers and educational partners is a crucial component that affects both the success of the instruction program and the opportunities for the library to make a positive impact on student learning.

Fostering a Culture of Inclusivity and Openness

Finally, the future should include a world where the library's teaching efforts are open and accessible for all. As Shulman (2000) writes, the collective enterprise of teaching should be communal, with the shared goal of changing teaching from "private property to community property" (p. 9). Due to their commitment to open access, academic libraries are in a unique position to make teaching and learning freely accessible and public, and, logically, this work happens within the instruction program. This also serves as a method for positioning teaching and learning as a true community of practice. As Reed (2018) notes, "the practice of information literacy librarians has been deeply impacted by educational theory, instructional design, and the scholarship of teaching and learning, resulting in a growing emphasis on learning outcomes and assessment" (p. 73), which results in an increased focus on issues related to scholarly communications and information access at the intersection of students, faculty, and campus administrators. The ideal future includes librarians learning and growing alongside other instructors on campus, all united around a common goal of open and inclusive educational exploration and innovation.

An academic library's instruction program reflects and communicates its vision for teaching and learning within the context of its institution, and the Instruction Coordinator plays an essential role in shaping and advancing this vision. Instruction Coordinators in academic libraries may have a variety of titles, but they face many of the same challenges in developing, promoting, and evaluating their instruction programs. This book has shared techniques and resources for advancing a library's teaching and learning agenda, including planning an instruction program, creating a mission and vision statement for the program, marketing and advocating for the library's teaching efforts, and creating an inclusive community of teachers within the library. While an instruction program can take many different shapes and sizes (from formal to informal and from small to large), it is a crucial and necessary component for positioning the library as a comprehensive and integral leader of teaching and learning on campus.

Appendix

An Instruction Coordinator's Bookshelf

LIBRARY INSTRUCTION

Accardi, M., Drabinski, E., & Kumbier, A. (Eds.). (2010). *Critical library instruction: Theories and methods*. Duluth, MN: Library Juice Press.

Booth, C. (2011). *Reflective teaching, effective learning: Instructional literacy for library educators*. Chicago, IL: American Library Association.

Grassian, E. S., & Kaplowitz, J. R. (2005). *Learning to lead and manage information literacy instruction programs*. New York, NY: Neal-Schuman Publishers.

Mader, S., & Gibson, C. (2019). *Building teaching and learning communities: Creating shared meaning and purpose*. Chicago, IL: American Library Association.

Mallon, M. N., Hays, L., Bradley, C., Huisman, R., & Belanger, J. (Eds.). (2019). *The grounded instruction librarian: Participating in the scholarship of teaching and learning*. Chicago, IL: American Library Association.

Miller, R. K., & Benjes-Small, C. M. (2016). *The new instruction librarian: A workbook for trainers and learners*. Chicago, IL: American Library Association.

Noe, N. W. (2013). *Creating and maintaining an information literacy instruction program in the twenty-first century: An ever changing landscape*. Oxford, UK: Chandos Publishing.

TEACHING AND LEARNING BEYOND LIBRARIES

Bain, K. (2011). *What the best college teachers do*. Cambridge, MA: Harvard University Press.

Green, E. (2014). *Building a better teacher: How teaching works (and how to teach it to everyone)*. New York, NY: W. W. Norton.

hooks, b. (1994). *Teaching to transgress: Education as the practice of freedom*. London, UK: Routledge.

Huston, T. (2009). *Teaching what you don't know*. Cambridge, MA: Harvard University Press.

Lang, J. M. (2010). *On course: A week-by-week guide to your first semester of college teaching*. Cambridge, MA: Harvard University Press.

Palmer, P. J. (2009). *The courage to teach: Exploring the inner landscape of a teacher's life*. San Francisco, CA: Jossey-Bass.

Shulman, L. S. (2004). *Teaching as community property: Essays on higher education*. Hoboken, NJ: John Wiley & Sons.

KEEPING UP WITH HIGHER EDUCATION

Note: While URLs may change, and not all content on these sites is freely available, these resources provide excellent options for librarians looking to stay informed about higher education.

- *The Chronicle of Higher Education*, https://www.chronicle.com/
- *Inside Higher Ed*, https://www.insidehighered.com/
- *Times Higher Education*, https://www.timeshighereducation.com/academic/news

CONTINUING EDUCATION AND PROFESSIONAL NETWORKS

The following list of selected associations, training, and professional networking resources are excellent sources for new and experienced instruction librarians looking to grow their network and pedagogical skills. A selected list of academic library and higher education conferences are listed in Chapter 9.

- *ACRL Framework for Information Literacy Toolkit*, https://acrl.libguides.com/framework/toolkit
- *ACRL Immersion Program*, http://www.ala.org/acrl/conferences/immersion
- *ACRL Instruction Section ILI-L Discussion List*, https://acrl.ala.org/IS/about-is-2/faq/ili-l-information-literacy-instruction-discussion-list/
- *Critical Librarianship and Pedagogy Symposium*, https://repository.arizona.edu/handle/10150/631129
- *EDUCAUSE*, https://www.educause.edu/
- *International Society for Exploring Teaching and Learning*, http://www.isetl.org/
- *Leadership Institute for Academic Librarians (Harvard's Graduate School of Education)*, https://www.gse.harvard.edu/ppe/program/leadership-institute-academic-librarians
- *Library Juice Academy* (includes courses such as critical information literacy pedagogy and the Scholarship of Teaching & Learning), http://libraryjuiceacademy.com/
- *Professional and Organizational Development Network in Higher Education (POD)*, https://podnetwork.org/

References

Accardi, M. T. (2010). Teaching against the grain: Critical assessment in the library classroom. In A. Kumbier, E. Drabinski, & M. T. Accardi (Eds.), *Critical library instruction: Theories and methods* (pp. 251–264). Duluth, MN: Library Juice Press.

Affleck, M. A. (1996). Burnout among bibliographic instruction librarians. *Library & Information Science Research, 18*, 169–172.

Alabi, J., & Weare, W. H. (2013). The power of observation: How librarians can benefit from the peer review of teaching even without a formal PROT program. *Georgia International Conference on Information Literacy*, 1. Retrieved from https://digitalcommons.georgiasouthern.edu/gaintlit/2013/2013/1

Alexander, L., & Bradley, D. R. (2010). Library instruction in a new culture of teaching and learning. *LOEX Conference Proceedings*. Retrieved from https://commons.emich.edu/cgi/viewcontent.cgi?referer=https://www.google.com/&httpsredir=1&article=1020&context=loexconf2010

Alire, C. A. (2007). Resonant leadership in academic libraries. In P. Hernon, J. R. Giesecke, & C. A. Alire (Eds.), *Academic librarians as emotionally intelligent leaders* (pp. 95–105). Westport, CT: Libraries Unlimited.

Ammons-Stephens, S., Cole, H. J., Jenkins-Gibbs, K., Riehle, C. F., & Weare Jr., W. H. (2009). Developing core leadership competencies for the library profession. *Library Leadership & Management 23*(2), 63–74.

Amsberry, D., Benjes-Small, C., Harrington, S., Miller, S., Mlinar, C., & Wetzel Wilkinson, C. (2017, April 28). *Roles and Strengths of Teaching Librarians*. Chicago, IL: Association of College and Research Libraries. Retrieved from http://www.ala.org/acrl/standards/teachinglibrarians

Angelo, T. A. (1995). Reassessing (and defining) assessment. *AAHE Bulletin , 48*(3), 7.

Archambault, S. G., & Masunaga, J. (2015). Curriculum mapping as a strategic planning tool. *Journal of Library Administration, 55*(6), 503–519.

Arellano Douglas, V. (2019, June 12). Innovating against a brick wall: Rebuilding the structures that shape our teaching. TILC 2019 Keynote [Blog post]. *Libraries + Inquiry*. Retrieved from https://veronicaarellanodouglas.com/critlib/innovating-against-a-brick-wall-rebuilding-the-structures-that-shape-our-teaching-tilc-2019-keynote/

Arellano Douglas, V., & Gadsby, J. (2017). Gendered labor and library instruction coordinators: The undervaluing of feminized work. In D. M. Mueller (Ed.), *At the helm: Leading transformation: The proceedings of the ACRL 2017 conference, March 22–25, 2017, Baltimore, Maryland* (pp. 266–274). Chicago, IL: Association of College and Research Libraries.

Arellano Douglas, V., & Gadsby, J. (2019, July 10). All carrots, no sticks: Relational practice and library instruction coordination. *In the library with a lead pipe*. Retrieved from http://

inthelibrarywiththeleadpipe.org/2019/all-carrots-no-sticks-relational-practice-and-library-instruction-coordination/

Association of College and Research Libraries. (2011). *Guidelines for instruction programs in academic libraries*. Retrieved from http://www.ala.org/acrl/standards/guidelinesinstruction

Association of College and Research Libraries. (2012). *Diversity standards: Cultural competency for academic libraries*. Retrieved from http://www.ala.org/acrl/standards/diversity

Association of College and Research Libraries. (2015). *Framework for information literacy for higher education* . Retrieved from http://www.ala.org/acrl/standards/ilframework

Association of College and Research Libraries. (2018). *Standards for libraries in higher education*. Retrieved from http://www.ala.org/acrl/standards/standardslibraries

Association of College and Research Libraries. (2019). *Characteristics of programs of information literacy that illustrate best practices: A guideline*. Retrieved from http://www.ala.org/acrl/standards/characteristics

Association of College and Research Libraries Instruction Section. (2018, January). *Research agenda for library instruction and information literacy*. Retrieved from https://acrl.ala.org/IS/instruction-tools-resources-2/professional-development/research-agenda-for-library-instruction-and-information-literacy/

Bahls, S. C. (2016, January 24). What leaders can learn from teaching undergraduates. *Chronicle of Higher Education, (62)*20. Retrieved from https://www.chronicle.com/article/What-Leaders-Can-Learn-From/235011

Bandy, J. (2017). Peer review of teaching. *Vanderbilt University*. Retrieved from https://cft.vanderbilt.edu/guides-sub-pages/peer-review-of-teaching/

Barradell, S., & Kennedy-Jones, M. (2015). Threshold concepts, student learning and curriculum: Making connections between theory and practice. *Innovations in Education and Teaching International, 52*(5), 536–545; doi: 10.1080/14703297.2013.866592

Bass, R. (1999). The scholarship of teaching: What's the problem. *Inventio: Creative Thinking About Learning and Teaching , 1*(1), 1–10. Retrieved from http://wiki.biologyscholars.org/@api/deki/files/2206/=15_RR_Assignment_2_Readings.pdf

Bass, R., & Eynon, B. (1998). Teaching culture, learning culture, and new media technologies: An introduction and framework. *Works and Days, 31/32*(1–2), 11–96.

International Federation of Library Associations and Institutions. Beacons of the information society: The Alexandria proclamation on information literacy and lifelong learning. (2005). Retrieved from https://www.ifla.org/publications/beacons-of-the-information-society-the-alexandria-proclamation-on-information-literacy

Becker, K. A. (1993). The characteristics of bibliographic instruction in relation to the causes of burnout. *Reference Quarterly, 32*(3), 346–57.

Beilin, I. (2015, February 25). Beyond the threshold: Conformity, resistance, and the ACRL Information Literacy Framework for Higher Education. *In the Library with the Lead Pipe*. Retrieved from http://www.inthelibrarywiththeleadpipe.org/2015/beyond-the-threshold-conformity-resistance-and-the-aclr-information-literacy-framework-for-higher-education/#footnote_11_6254

Benjes-Small, C., & Miller, R. K. (2017). *The new instruction librarian: A workbook for trainers and learners*. Chicago, IL: American Library Association.

Bennett, M. H. (2011). The benefits of non-library professional organization membership for liaison librarians. *Journal of Academic Librarianship, 37*(1), 46–53. https://doi.org/10.1016/j.acalib.2010.10.006

Blakesley, E., & Baron, L. S. (2002). Leading information literacy programs. *Journal of Library Administration, 36*(1–2), 143–165. DOI: 10.1300/J111v36n01_09

Bolman, L. G., & Deal, T. E. (1991). *Reframing organizations: Artistry, choice, and leadership*. San Francisco, CA: Jossey-Bass.

Bolman, L. G., & Gallos, J. V. (2011). *Reframing academic leadership*. San Francisco, CA: Wiley.

Booth, C. (2011). *Reflective teaching, effective learning: Instructional literacy for library educators*. Chicago, IL: American Library Association.

Booth, C., Brecher, D., Lowe, M. S., Stone, S., & Tagge, N. (2014). Visual curriculum mapping template. *Curriculum Maps.* 52. Retrieved from https://scholarship.claremont.edu/ccct_cmaps/52/

Bowles-Terry, M. (2012). Library instruction and academic success: A mixed-methods assessment of a library instruction program. *Evidence Based Library and Information Practice, 7*(1), 82–95. Retrieved from https://repository.uwyo.edu/libraries_facpub/8/

Bransford, J. D., Brown, A. L., & Cocking, R. R. (2000). Learning: From speculation to science. In J. D. Bransford, A. L. Brown, & R. R. Cocking (Eds.), *How people learn: Brain, mind, experience, and school* (pp. 3–27). Washington, DC: National Academies Press.

Brown, B. (2018). *Dare to lead: Brave work. Tough conversations. Whole hearts.* New York, NY: Random House.

Bruch, C., & Wilkinson, C. W. (2012). Surveying terrain, clearing pathways. In C. W. Wilkinson & C. Bruch (Eds.), *Transforming information literacy programs: Intersecting frontiers of self, library culture, and campus community* (pp. 3–44). Chicago, IL: Association of College & Research Libraries.

Buchanan, H., Webb, K. K., Houk, A. H., & Tingelstad, C. (2015). Curriculum mapping in academic libraries. *New Review of Academic Librarianship, 21*(1), 94–111.

Bundy, A. (Ed.). (2004). Australian and New Zealand information literacy framework (2nd ed.). Retrieved from http://www.caul.edu.au/content/upload/files/info-literacy/InfoLiteracy-Framework.pdf

Caniëls, M. C. J., Semejin, J. H., & Renders, I. H. M. (2018). Mind the mindset! The interaction of proactive personality, transformational leadership and growth mindset for engagement at work. *Career Development International, 23*(1), 48–66. DOI 10.1108/CDI-11-2016-0194

Carroll, A. J., & Klipfel, K. M. (2019). Talent, schmalent: An instructional design/action research framework for the professionalization of teaching in academic libraries. *Journal of Academic Librarianship, 45,* 110–118.

Castro Gessner, A. G., & Eldemire, E. (2015). Laying the groundwork for information literacy at a research university. *Performance Measurement and Metrics, 16*(1), 4–17.

Cater-Steel, A., McDonald, J., Albion, P., & Redmond, P. (2017). Sustaining the momentum: A cross-institutional community of practice for research supervisors. In J. McDonald & A. Cater-Steel (Eds.), *Implementing Communities of Practice in Higher Education* (pp. 3–17). Singapore: Springer.

Center for Teaching. (2019). *Teaching statements.* Vanderbilt University Center for Teaching. Retrieved from https://cft.vanderbilt.edu/guides-sub-pages/teaching-statements/

Chapman, J. M., Pettway, C., & White, M. (2001). The portfolio: An instruction program assessment tool. *Reference Services Review, 29*(4), 294–300. https://doi.org/10.1108/EUM0000000006491

Charles, L. H. (2015). Using an informational literacy curriculum map as a means of communication and accountability for stakeholders in higher education. *Journal of Information Literacy, 9*(1), 47–61. https://doi.org/10.11645/9.1.1959

Chodock, T., & Dolinger, E. (2009). Applying Universal Design to information literacy: Teaching students who learn differently at Landmark College. *Reference & User Services Quarterly, 49,* 24–32. https://doi.org/10.5860/rusq.49n1.24

Chow, A., & Rich, M. (2013). The ideal qualities and tasks of library leaders: Perspectives of academic, public, school, and special library administrators. *Library Leadership & Management, 27*(1/2).

Clark, M., Vardeman, K., & Barba, S. (2014). Perceived inadequacy: A study of imposter phenomenon among college and research librarians. *College & Research Libraries, 75*(3), 255–271.

Colborn, N. W., & Cordell, R. M. (1998). Moving from subjective to objective assessments of your instruction program. *Reference Services Review, 26*(3/4), 125–137. https://doi.org/10.1108/00907329810307821

College of Business Administration. (2016, July 29). *Assessment guide for academic programs.* Texas A&M University Central Texas. Retrieved from https://www.tamuct.edu/coba/docs/coba-assessment-guide.pdf

Cooke, N. (2012). Professional development 2.0 for librarians: Developing an online personal learning network (PLN). *Library Hi Tech News*, *29*(3), 1–9. DOI 10.1108/07419051211241840

Corrall, S. (2007). Benchmarking strategic engagement with information literacy in higher education: Towards a working model. *Information Research*, *12*(4), paper 328. Retrieved from http://InformationR.net/ir/12-4/paper328.html

Costin, K., & Morgan, P. (2019). Moving from the sidelines to the playing field: Developing relationship with student athletics. *College & Research Libraries News*, *80*(4), 224.

Cranton, P. (2001). *Becoming an authentic teacher in higher education*. Malabar, FL: Krieger Publishing.

Curtis, R. (2016). Information literacy advocates: Developing student skills through a peer support approach. *Health Information & Libraries Journal*, *33*, 334–339. doi:10.1111/hir.12156

Davis, E. L., Lundstrom, K., & Martin, P. N. (2011). Librarian perceptions and information literacy instruction models. *Reference Services Review*, *39*(4), 686–702. Retrieved from https://digitalcommons.usu.edu/lib_pubs/106

Donovan, C. (2009, August 19). Sense of self: Embracing your teacher identity. *In the Library with the Lead Pipe*. Retrieved from http://www.inthelibrarywiththeleadpipe.org/2009/sense-of-self-embracing-your-teacher-identity/

Doucette, W. C., & Tolley, R. L. (2017). Using civility in the form of mindful speech and action to cultivate empathy among library employees. In S. S. Hines & M. L. Matteson (Eds.), *Emotion in the workplace. Advances in Library Administration and Organization, Volume 37* (pp. 167–187). Bingley, UK: Emerald.

Duffus, L. (2004). The Personal Strategic Plan: A tool for career planning and advancement. *International Journal of Management*, *21*(2), 144–148.

Epper, R. M. (1999). Applying benchmarking to higher education: Some lessons from experience. *Change: The Magazine of Higher Education*, *31*(6), 24–31. DOI:10.1080/00091389909604230

Edmondson, A. C. (2018). *The fearless organization: Creating psychological safety in the workplace for learning, innovation, and growth*. Hoboken, NJ: John Wiley & Sons.

Elliott, C. (2009). We are not alone: The power of Personal Learning Networks. *Synergy*, *7*(1), 47–50.

Evans, R. (2007). The authentic leader. In *The Jossey-Bass reader on educational leadership* (2nd ed.) (pp. 135–156). San Francisco, CA: Jossey Bass.

Falcone, A., & McCartin, L. (2018). Be critical, but be flexible: Using the Framework to facilitate student learning outcome development. *C&RL News*, *79*(1). Retrieved from https://crln.acrl.org/index.php/crlnews/article/view/16859/18479

Farkas, M. (2017, September 1). Framework freakout? Engaging with the Framework for Information Literacy. *American Libraries*. Retrieved from https://americanlibrariesmagazine.org/2017/09/01/framework-freakout/

Fister, B. (2014, May 22). Crossing thresholds and learning in libraries [Blog post]. *Library Babel Fish*. Retrieved from http://www.insidehighered.com/blogs/library-babel-fish/crossing-thresholds-and-learning-libraries#sthash.AsO9Tifm.dpbs

Fleming-May, R. A., & Douglass, K. (2014). Framing librarianship in the academy: An analysis using Bolman and Deal's model of organizations. *College & Research Libraries*, *75*(3), 389–415.

Fletcher, J. K. (1998). Relational practice: A feminist reconstruction of work. *Journal of Management Inquiry*, *7*(2), 163–187.

Foasberg, N. M. (2015). From standards to frameworks for IL: How the ACRL Framework addresses critiques of the standards. *portal: Libraries and the Academy*, *15*(4), 699–717.

Fowler, C. S., & Walter, S. (2003). Instructional leadership: New responsibilities for a new reality. *College & Research Libraries News*, *64*(7), 465–468.

Freedman, S., & Vreven, D. (2017). Workplace incivility and bullying in the library: Perception or reality? *College & Research Libraries*, *77*(6), 727–748.

Freiling, J., & Huth, S. (2005). Limitations and challenges of benchmarking: A competence based perspective. In R. Sanchez & A. Heene (Eds.), *Competence perspectives on managing interfirm interactions (Advances in Applied Business Strategy, Vol. 8)* (pp. 3–25). Bingly, UK: Emerald Group.

Galvin, J. (2005). Alternative strategies for promoting information literacy. *The Journal of Academic Librarianship, 31*(4), 352–357. https://doi.org/10.1016/j.acalib.2005.04.003

Gammons, R. W., & Inge, L. T. (2017). Using the ACRL Framework to develop a student centered model for program-level assessment. *Communications in Information Literacy, 11*(1), 168–184. https://doi.org/10.15760/comminfolit.2017.11.1.40

Garcia, E. V. (2016). Strategic planning: A tool for personal and career growth. *Heart Asia, 8*(1), 36–39. https://doi.org/10.1136/heartasia-2015-010684

Gerwitz, S. R. (2014). Evaluating an instruction program with various assessment measures. *Reference Services Review, 42*(1), 16–33. https://doi.org/10.1108/RSR-03-2013-0019

Gibson, C., & Jacobson, T. E. (2014). Informing and extending the draft ACRL Information Literacy Framework for Higher Education: An overview and avenues for research. *College & Research Libraries, 75*(3), 250–254.

Giesecke, J. R. (2007). Emotional intelligence. In P. Hernon, J. R. Giesecke, & C. A. Alire (Eds.), *Academic librarians as emotionally intelligent leaders* (pp. 1–10). Westport, CT: Libraries Unlimited.

Gold, M. L., & Grotti, M. G. (2013). Do job advertisements reflect ACRL's Standards for Proficiencies for Instruction Librarians and Coordinators?: A content analysis. *The Journal of Academic Librarianship, 39*(6), 558–565. https://doi.org/10.1016/j.acalib.2013.05.013

Goleman, D. (2005). *Working with emotional intelligence.* New York: Bantam Books.

Goleman, D., Boyatzis, R., & McKee, A. (2002). *Primal leadership: Realizing the power of emotional intelligence.* Boston, MA: Harvard Business School Press.

Grassian, E. (2017). Teaching and learning alternatives: A global overview. *Reference & User Services Quarterly, 56*(4), 232–239.

Grassian, E. S., & Kaplowitz, J. R. (2005). *Learning to lead and manage information literacy instruction.* New York, NY: Neal-Schuman Publishers.

Grassian, E. S., & Kaplowitz, J. R. (2001). *Information literacy instruction: Theory and practice.* New York: Neal-Schuman Publishers.

Greenleaf, R. K. (1977). *Servant leadership: A journey into the nature of legitimate power and greatness.* Indianapolis, IN: Paulist Press.

Guth, L. F., Arnold, J. M., Bielat, V. E., Perez-Stable, M. A., & Vander Meer, P. F. (2018). Faculty voices on the Framework: Implications for instruction and dialogue. *portal: Libraries & the Academy, 18*(4), 693–718.

Harland, F., Stewart, G., & Bruce, C. (2019). Leading the academic library in strategic engagement with stakeholders: A Constructivist grounded theory. *College & Research Libraries.*

Harwell, K. (2008). Burnout strategies for librarians. *Journal of Business & Finance Librarianship, 13*(3), 379–390. DOI:10.1080/08963560802183021

Haynie, A., Chick, N. L., & Gurung, R. A. R. (2009). From generic to signature pedagogies: Teaching disciplinary understandings. In A. Haynie, N. L. Chick, & R. A. R. Gurung (Eds.), *Exploring signature pedagogies: Approaches to teaching disciplinary habits of mind* (pp. 1–16). Sterling, VA: Stylus Publishing.

Head, A. J., & Brown, K. (1995). Reframing techniques and managing change within the library setting. *Journal of Library Administration, 22*(1), 1–12.

Henrich, K. J., & Attebury, R. (2010). Communities of practice at an academic library: A new approach to mentoring at the University of Idaho. *The Journal of Academic Librarianship, 36*(2), 158–165. https://doi.org/10.1016/j.acalib.2010.01.007

Hess, A. N. (2015). Equipping academic librarians to integrate the Framework into instructional practices: A theoretical application. *Journal of Academic Librarianship, 41*(6), 771–776.

Hinchliffe, L. J. (2016a, February 16). *Coordinator for information literacy services and instruction (aka my job).* Retrieved from https://lisahinchliffe.com/2016/02/16/coordinator-for-information-literacy/

Hinchliffe, L. J. (2016b). Information literacy leadership and program evaluation: Using a curriculum map for program development. Presented at Curriculum Mapping: A CARLI-Sponsored ACRL Preconference. Chicago, IL. Retrieved from http://hdl.handle.net/2142/89697

References

Hinojosa, J. C. (2012). Personal strategic plan development: Getting ready for changes in our professional and personal lives. *The American Journal of Occupational Therapy, 66*(3), 34–38.

Hoadley, C. (2014). What is a community of practice and how can we support it? In S. Land & D. Jonassen (Eds.), *Theoretical foundations of learning environments* (pp. 286–300). New York, NY: Taylor and Francis.

Hofer, A. R., Townsend, L., & Brunetti, K. (2012). Troublesome concepts and information literacy: Investigating threshold concepts for IL instruction. *portal: Libraries & the Academy, 12*(4), 387–405.

Hofer, A. R., & Townsend, L., & Brunetti, K. (2013). A threshold concepts approach to the Standards revision. *Communications in Information Literacy, 7*(2), 108–113. https://doi.org/10.15760/comminfolit.2013.7.2.141

Hovious, A. (2015, January 1). ACRL Standards: Aligning the current with the proposed [Blog post]. *Designer Librarian*. Retrieved from https://designerlibrarian.wordpress.com/2015/01/21/acrl-standards-aligning-the-current-with-the-proposed/

Hunt, F., & Birks, J. (2004). Best practices in information literacy. *portal: Libraries and the Academy, 4*(1), 27–39.

Hutchings, P. (1996). Building a new culture of teaching and learning. *About Campus, 1*(5), 4–8. https://doi.org/10.1002/abc.6190010502

Hutchings, P. (2000). *Introduction to opening lines: Approaches to the scholarship of teaching and learning*. San Francisco, CA: Jossey-Bass.

"Information Literacy Plan based on ACRL's Framework for Information Literacy for Higher Education." (2018, May 8). Milligan Libraries. Retrieved from https://library.milligan.edu/information-literacy-frameworks/

Jacobs, H. L. M. (2016). Falling out of praxis: Reflection as a pedagogical habit of mind. In N. Pagowsky & K. McElroy (Eds.), *Critical library pedagogy handbook, Volume 1* (pp. 1–8). Chicago, IL: Association of College and Research Libraries.

Jacobson, T. E., & Gibson, C. (2015). First thoughts on implementing the Framework for Information Literacy. *Communications in Information Literacy, 9*(2), 102–110.

Jaguszewski, J., & Williams, K. (2013). *New roles for new times: Transforming liaison roles in research libraries*. Retrieved from http://conservancy.umn.edu/handle/11299/169867

Jankowski, N. A., & Marshall, D. W. (2017). *Degrees that matter: Moving higher education to a learning systems paradigm*. Stering, VA: Stylus Publishing.

Johnson-Grau, G., Archambault, S. G., Acosta, E. S., & McLean, L. (2016). Patience, persistence, and process: Embedding a campus-wide information literacy program across the curriculum. *The Journal of Academic Librarianship, 42*(6), 750–756. https://doi.org/10.1016/j.acalib.2016.10.013

Julien, H., Gross, M., & Latham, D. (2018). Survey of information literacy instructional practices in U.S. academic libraries. *College & Research Libraries, 79*(2), 179–199. doi:10.5860/crl.79.2.179

Julien, H., & Pecoskie, J. L. (2009). Librarians' experiences of the teaching role: Grounded in campus relationships. *Library & Information Science Research, 31*(3): 149–154. DOI: https://doi.org/10.1016/j.lisr.2009.03.005

Kendrick, K. D. (2017). The low morale experience of academic librarians: A phenomenological study. *Journal of Library Administration, 57*(8), 846–878.

Kenney, A. R. (2014). Leveraging the liaison model: From defining 21st century research libraries to implementing 21st century research universities. *Ithaka S+R*. Retrieved from https://sr.ithaka.org/blog/leveraging-the-liaison-model-from-defining-21st-century-research-libraries-to-implementing-21st-century-research-universities/

Kim, J-A. (2015). Integrating communities of practice into library services. *Collaborative Librarianship, 7*(2), 47–55.

Kinzie, J., Hutchings, P., & Jankowski, N. A. (2015). Fostering greater use of assessment results: Principles for effective practice. In G. D. Kuh, S. O. Ikenberry, N. A. Jankowski, T.R. Cain, P. T. Ewell, P. Hutchings, & J. Kinsie (Eds.), *Using evidence of student learning* (pp. 51–72). San Francisco, CA: Jossey-Bass.

Krautter, M. (2013). Advocating for the devil: Transforming conflict in libraries. In D. M. Mueller (Ed.), *Imagine, Innovate, Inspire: Proceedings of the ACRL 2013 Conference* (pp. 9–15). Chicago, IL: Association of College and Research Libraries.

Kreitz, P. A. (2009). Leadership and emotional intelligence: A study of university library directors and their senior management teams. *College & Research Libraries, (70)*6, 531–554.

Kubicek, J. (2012). Intentional leadership. *Leader to Leader, 2012*(64), 38–43. https://doi:10.1002/ltl.20021

Kuh, G. D., Ikenberry, S. O., Jankowski, N. A., Reese Cain, T., Ewell, P. T., Hutchings, P., & Kinzie, J. (2015). Beyond compliance: Making assessment matter. *Change: The Magazine of Higher Learning, 47*(5), 8–17. doi: 10.1080/00091383.2015.1077661

Kustra, E., Meadows, K.N., Dawson, D., Dishke Hondzel, C., Goff, L., Wolf, P., ... Hughes, S. E. (2014). *Teaching culture indicators: Enhancing quality teaching.* Retrieved from http://www.uwindsor.ca/ctl/sites/uwindsor.ca.ctl/files/teaching_culture_indicators.pdf

Lankes, R. D. (2016). *The new librarianship field guide.* Cambridge, MA: MIT Press.

Laursen, P. (2005). The authentic teacher. In D. Beijaard, P. Meijer, G. Morine-Dershimer, & H. Tillema (Eds.), *Teacher professional development in changing conditions* (pp. 199–212). New York, NY: Springer.

Lave, J., & Wenger, E. (1991). *Situated learning: Legitimate peripheral participation.* Cambridge, UK: Cambridge University Press.

Lo, L. S., & Herman, B. (2017). An investigation of factors impacting the wellness of academic library employees. *College & Research Libraries, 78*(5), 789–811. doi:10.5860/crl.78.6.789

Lucas, U., & Mladenovic, R. (2007). The potential of threshold concepts: An emerging framework for educational research and practice. *London Review of Education, 5*(3), 237–248. https://doi.org/10.1080/14748460701661294

Lüdert, J. (n.d.). *Signature pedagogy and threshold concepts.* Retrieved March 2019 from https://blogs.ubc.ca/janluedert/signature-pedagogy-and-treshold-concepts/

Lyle, H., Fournier, J., Phuwanartnurak, A., Lewis, J., & Roberts, K. (2016, March). Connecting students with co-curricular experiences: A case study from the University of Washington. *EDUCAUSE SEI Case Study.* Retrieved from https://library.educause.edu/-/media/files/library/2016/3/sei1601.pdf

Mader, S. (1996). Instruction librarians: Leadership in the new organization. *Research Quarterly, 36*(2), 192–197.

Mader, S. B., & Gibson, C. (2019 October). *Learning in partnership.* Urbana, IL: University of Illinois and Indiana University, National Institute for Learning Outcomes Assessment (NILOA). Retrieved from https://www.learningoutcomesassessment.org/wp-content/uploads/2019/10/Viewpoint-MaderGibson.pdf

Mader, S. B., & Gibson, C. (2019). Teaching and learning centers: Recasting the role of librarians as educators and change agents. *ACRL Conference Proceedings.* Retrieved from http://www.ala.org/acrl/sites/ala.org.acrl/files/content/conferences/confsandpreconfs/2019/TeachingandLearningCenters.pdf

Mallon, M. N. (2018). *The pivotal role of academic librarians in digital learning.* Santa Barbara, CA: Libraries Unlimited/ABC-CLIO.

Mallon, M. N., & Smiley, B. L. (2019, April). *Fostering the development of teaching identity with communities of practice.* Poster session presented at the Association of College & Research Libraries Conference, Cleveland, OH.

Mårtensson, K., Roxå, T,. & Olsson, T. (2011). Developing a quality culture through the Scholarship of Teaching and Learning. *Higher Education Research & Development, 30*(1), 51–62. DOI: 10.1080/07294360.2011.536972

Martinez, J., & Forrey, M. (2019). Overcoming imposter syndrome: The adventures of two new instruction librarians. *Reference Services Review.* Advance online publication. doi 10.1108/RSR-03-2019-0021

Maslach, C., & Jackson, S. E. (1981). The measurement of experienced burnout. *Journal of Occupational Behavior, 2,* 99–113.

Mata, H., Latham, T. P., & Ransome, Y. (2010). Benefits of professional organization membership and participation in national conferences: Considerations for students and new professionals. *Health Promotion Practice, 11*(4), 450–453. DOI: 10.1177/1524839910370427

Mathuews, K. (2016). Moving beyond diversity to social justice: A call to action for academic libraries. *Progressive Librarian, 44*, 6–27.

Maxwell, J. C. (2005). *The 360-degree leader: Developing your influence from anywhere in the organization*. Nashville, TN: Thomas Nelson.

McClenney, K. M. (2006), Benchmarking effective educational practice. *New Directions for Community Colleges, 134*, 47–55. doi:10.1002/cc.236

McKee, A., Johnston, F., & Massimilian, R. (2006). Mindfulness, hope and compassion: A leader's road map to renewal. *Ivey Business Journal (Online)*, 1–5.

McNiff, L., & Hays, L. (2017). SoTL in the LIS classroom: Helping future academic librarians become more engaged teachers. *Communications in Information Literacy, 11*(2), 366–377. https://doi.org/10.15760/comminfolit.2017.11.2.8

Messersmith, B. (2015, April 22). Adopting the educator's mindset: Charting new paths in curriculum and assessment mapping. *In the Library with the Lead Pipe*. Retrieved from http://www.inthelibrarywiththeleadpipe.org/2015/adopting-the-educators-mindset-charting-new-paths-in-curriculum-and-assessment-mapping/

Meyer, J. H.F. (2008). *Threshold concepts within the disciplines*. Boston, MA: Sense Publishers.

Meyer, J., & Land, R. (2003). Threshold concepts and troublesome knowledge: Linkages to ways of thinking and practising within the disciplines. *Occasional Report No. 4*. Retrieved from http://www.etl.tla.ed.ac.uk/docs/ETLreport4.pdf

Miller-Young, J. E., Anderson, C., Kiceniuk, D., Mooney, J., Riddell, J., Schmidt Hanbidge, A., . . . Chick, N. (2017). Leading up in the Scholarship of Teaching and Learning. *The Canadian Journal for the Scholarship of Teaching and Learning, 8*(2). Retrieved from https://doi.org/10.5206/cjsotl-rcacea.2017.2.4

National Institute for Learning Outcomes Assessment. (2018, December). *Mapping learning: A toolkit*. Urbana, IL: University of Illinois and Indiana University. Retrieved from http://www.learningoutcomesassessment.org/documents/Mapping%20Learning.pdf

Nims, J. K. (1999). Marketing library instruction services: Changes and trends. *Reference Services Review, 27*(3), 249–253.

Noe, N. (2013). *Creating and maintaining an information literacy instruction program in the twenty-first century*. Oxford, UK: Chandos Publishing.

Norbury, L. (2001). Peer observation of teaching: A method for improving teaching quality. *New Review of Academic Librarianship, 7*(1), 87–99.

Nussbaum-Beach, S. (2012/2013). Just the facts: Personal learning networks. *Educational Horizons, 91*(2), 26–27.

Oakleaf, M. (2010). *The value of academic libraries: A comprehensive research review and report*. Chicago, IL: Association of College and Research Libraries, American Library Association.

Owusu-Ansah, E. K. (2004). Information literacy and higher education: Placing the academic library in the center of a comprehensive solution. *Journal of Academic Librarianship, 30*(1), 3–16. https://doi.org/10.1016/j.jal.2003.11.002

Pagowsky, N. (2019, June 10). *Information literacy frames and student learning outcomes*. University of Arizona Libraries' instruction program. Retrieved from https://libguides.library.arizona.edu/instruction

Palmer, P. J. (1998). *The courage to teach: Exploring the inner landscape of a teacher's life*. San Francisco, CA: Jossey-Bass.

Parkman, A. (2016). The imposter phenomenon in higher education: Incidence and impact. *Journal of Higher Education Theory and Practice, 16*(1), 51–60.

Parry, J. (2008). Librarians do fly: Strategies for staying aloft. *Library Management, 29*(1/2), 41–50.

Patterson, C. D., & Howell, D. W. (1990). Library user education: Assessing the attitudes of those who teach. *Research Quarterly, 29*(4), 513–524.

Pemberton, A. (2010). Needs analysis: The first step in library instruction assessment. *Georgia International Conference on Information Literacy*, 8. Retrieved from https://digitalcommons.georgiasouthern.edu/gaintlit/2010/2010/8

Pettas, W., & Gilliland, S. L. (1992). Conflict in the large academic library: Friend or foe? *Journal of Academic Librarianship*, *18*(1), 24–29.

Plocharczyk, L. (2007). On organizational conflict: Reaping the benefits of effective conflict management. *Journal of Access Services*, *4*(1–2), 85–120.

Porter, B. (2010). Managing with emotional intelligence. *Library Leadership & Management*, *24*(4), 199–201.

Portland State University Library. (n.d.). *Library instruction program learning outcomes.* Portland State University. Retrieved from https://library.pdx.edu/wp-content/uploads/library_instruction_outcomes.pdf

Program Goals. (n.d.). *Waidner-Spahr Library information literacy program.* Retrieved from https://www.dickinson.edu/info/20391/library/2550/information_literacy_program/2

Pyrko, I., Dörfler, V., & Eden, C. (2017). Thinking together: What Communities of Practice work? *Human Relations, 70*(4), 389–409. DOI 10.1177/0018726716661040

Reed, M. (2018). Creating learning opportunities in open education: An exploration of the intersections of information literacy and scholarly communication. In A. Wesolek, J. Lashley, & A. Langley (Eds.), *OER: A field guide for academic librarians* (pp. 73–92). Forest Grove, OR: Pacific University Press.

Richmond, L (2017). A feminist critique of servant leadership. In S. Lew & B. Yousefi (Eds.), *Feminists among us: Resistance and advocacy in library leadership* (pp. 43–66). Sacramento, CA: Library Juice Press.

Roxå, T., Mårtensson, K., & Alveteg, M. (2011). Understanding and influencing teaching and learning cultures at university: A network approach. *Higher Education*, *62*(1), 99–111.

Rzheuskyi, A., & Kunanets N. (2018). The concept of benchmarking in librarianship. Paper 187. *CEUR Workshop Proceedings, 2104*, 45–57. Retrieved from http://ceur-ws.org/Vol-2104/paper_187.pdf

Salovey, P., & Mayer, J. D. (1990). Emotional intelligence. *Imagination, Cognition, and Personality, 9*(3), 185–211.

Saunders, L. (2011). Librarians as teacher leaders: Definitions, challenges, and opportunities. In D. M. Muller (Ed.), *ACRL 2011 Conference Papers* (pp. 264–274). Chicago, IL: Association of College and Research Libraries.

Schulte, J., Tiffen, B., Edwards, J., Abbott, S., & Luca, E. (2018). Shaping the future of academic libraries: Authentic learning for the next generation. *College & Research Libraries, 79*(5), 685–696.

SCONUL Working Group on Information Literacy. (2011). *The SCONUL seven pillars of information literacy: A core model for higher education.* Retrieved from https://www.sconul.ac.uk/sites/default/files/documents/coremodel.pdf

Scott, K. (2017). *Radical candor: Be a kick-ass boss without losing your humanity.* New York, NY: St. Martin's Press.

Scott, S. S., Mcguire, J. M., & Shaw, S. F. (2003). Universal design for instruction: A new paradigm for adult instruction in postsecondary education. *Remedial and Special Education, 24*(6), 369–379.

Senge, P. M. (1990). The leader's new work: Building learning organizations. *Sloan Management Review, 32*(1), 7–22.

Seymour, C. (2012). Ethnographic study of information literacy librarians' work experience: A report from two states. In C. W. Wilkinson & C. Bruch (Eds.), *Transforming information literacy programs: Intersecting frontiers of self, library culture, and campus community* (pp. 45–71). Chicago, IL: Association of College & Research Libraries.

Sheesley, D. F. (2001). Burnout and the academic teaching librarian: An examination of the problem and suggested solutions. *The Journal of Academic Librarianship*, *27*(6), 447–451.

Shulman, L. S. (2000). *Fostering a scholarship of teaching and learning* (Report No. HE 033018). Athens, GA: Institute of Higher Education. (ERIC Document Reproduction Service No. ED442420)

Shulman, L. (2005). Signature pedagogies in the professions. *Daedalus, 134*(3), 52–59.

Sonntag, G. (2007). In search of excellence: Qualities of a library teaching model. In S. C. Curzon & L. D. Lampert (Eds.), *Proven strategies for building an information literacy program* (133–146). New York, NY: Neal-Schuman.

Sowell, S. (2014). Building a new paradigm: Analysis of a case study in organizational change in collection management using Bolman's and Deal's four-frame model. *Collection Management*, *39*(2–3), 211–226.

Spears, L. C. (1998). Tracing the growing impact of servant-leadership. In L. C. Spears (Ed.), *Insights on leadership: Service, stewardship, spirit, and servant-leadership* (pp. 1–12). New York, NY: John Wiley & Sons.

St. Clair, G. (2006). Benchmarking and restructuring. *American Library Association.* Retrieved from http://www.ala.org/acrl/publications/booksanddigitalresources/booksmonographs/pil/pil49/stclair

Stassen, M. L. A., Doherty, K., & Poe, M. (2001). *Program-based review and assessment: Tools and techniques for program improvement.* Office of Academic Planning and Assessment: University of Massachusetts Amherst. Retrieved from http://www.umass.edu/oapa/sites/default/files/pdf/handbooks/program_assessment_handbook.pdf

Tancheva, K., Andrews, C., & Steinhart, G. S. (2007). Library instruction assessment in academic libraries. *Public Services Quarterly*, *3*(1/2), 29–56. http://dx.doi.org/10.1300/J295v03n01_03

Tewell, E. (2018). The practice and promise of critical information literacy: Academic librarians' involvement in critical library instruction. *College & Research Libraries*, *79*(1), 10–34. doi:10.5860/crl.79.1.10

Tomaszewski, R., & MacDonald, K. I. (2009). Identifying subject-specific conferences as professional development opportunities for the academic librarian. *The Journal of Academic Librarianship*, *35*(6), 583–590. https://doi.org/10.1016/j.acalib.2009.08.006

Tysick, C. (2002). Attending conferences outside of librarianship. *College & Undergraduate Libraries*, *9*(2), 75–81. DOI: 10.1300/J106v09n02_08

USC Libraries. (n.d.). *Information literacy outcomes for undergraduates.* Retrieved from https://libraries.usc.edu/research/instructional-services/learning-outcomes

Walter, S. (2015). What librarians can learn from the study of college teaching. *ACRL Conference Proceedings.* Retrieved from http://www.ala.org/acrl/sites/ala.org.acrl/files/content/conferences/pdf/waltr05.pdf

Webb, K., & Hoover, J. (2015). Universal Design for Learning (UDL) in the academic library: A methodology for mapping multiple means of representation in library tutorials. *College & Research Libraries*, *76*(4), 537–553. https://doi.org/10.5860/crl.76.4.537

Weiner, S. A. (2012). Institutionalizing information literacy. *The Journal of Academic Librarianship*, *38*(5), 287–293. https://doi.org/10.1016/j.acalib.2012.05.004

Wells, M., & Young, R. (1994). Making your move and getting it right. *Special Libraries*, *85*(3), 145–53.

Wenger, E. (1998). *Communities of practice: Learning, meaning, and identity.* Cambridge: Cambridge University Press.

Wenger, E. (2002). *Quick start-up guide for Communities of Practice.* Retrieved from https://wenger-trayner.com/project/community-of-practice-start-up-guide/

Wheeler, E., & McKinney, P. (2015). Are librarians teachers? Investigating academic librarians' perceptions of their own teaching skills. *Journal of Information Literacy*, *9*(2), 111–128. https://doi.org/10.11645/9.2.1985

Wilkinson, L. (2014, June 19). The problem with threshold concepts [Blog post]. *Sense and Reference: A Philosophical Library Blog.* Retrieved from https://senseandreference.wordpress.com/2014/06/19/the-problem-with-threshold-concepts/

Willey, M. (2014). Library instructor development and cultivating a community of practice. *Advances in Librarianship*, *38*, 83–100.

Witkin, B. R., & Altschuld, J. W. (1995). *Planning and conducting a needs assessment: A practical guide.* Thousand Oaks, CA: Sage.

Wood, S., Dukewich, K., & Denton, A. W. (2016). Promoting pedagogy: The development of a teaching & learning CoP in a research-focused department. *Transformative Dialogues: Teaching & Learning Journal*, *9*(1).

Zald, A. E., & Gilchrist, D. (2008). Instruction and program design through assessment. In C. N. Cox & E. B. Lindsay (Eds.), *Information literacy instruction handbook* (pp. 164–192). Chicago, IL: Association of College and Research Libraries. American Library Association. Retrieved from https://digitalscholarship.unlv.edu/lib_articles/146

Zald, A. E., & Millet, M. (2012). Hitching your wagon to institutional goals. In C. W. Wilkinson & C. Bruch (Eds.), *Transforming information literacy programs: Intersecting frontiers of self, library culture, and campus community* (pp. 119–130). Chicago, IL: Association of College & Research Libraries.

Index

accreditation, 23, 25, 26, 46, 66, 83, 84
administration, 6, 24, 28, 61, 66, 98, 102, 109. *See also* stakeholders
administrators, 2, 22, 86, 89, 98, 100, 117; campus, 18, 23, 26, 51, 52, 66, 71, 84, 121; library, 8, 10, 22–23, 62, 64, 66, 70, 84, 86, 99, 106, 109, 111, 116, 118. *See also* stakeholders
advocacy, 10, 12, 61–62, 63, 65, 68, 69, 71–72, 118, 121; by faculty, 67; goals, 63–64, 67; an Instruction Coordinator's role in, 3, 4, 45, 54, 58, 71, 84; for instruction programs, xiii, xvii, 4, 26, 52, 59, 70, 89, 117; for librarians as teaching partners, x, 5, 29, 48, 65, 99. *See also* marketing
assessment, 22, 43, 58, 64, 70–71, 77, 90, 103; culture of, 6, 29; cycle of, 73–74, 84, 85; data collection, 28, 63, 67, 71, 85–87, 93; of Instruction Coordinators, 110, 111; of instruction programs, xiii, xvii, 2, 21, 22, 52, 66, 67, 74, 76, 77, 78, 79, 83, 85, 87, 89, 99; outcomes-based, 75, 83, 84, 106, 121; plans, 75, 77–78, 87, 111; needs analysis, 27, 59, 76, 117; of student learning, 5, 19, 20, 21, 26, 37, 38, 42, 43, 74, 79, 80–81, 83
Association of College & Research Libraries (ACRL): *Characteristics of Programs of Information Literacy that Illustrate Best Practices*, xiv; *Diversity Standards: Cultural Competency for Academic Libraries*, 58; *Guidelines for Instruction Programs in Academic Libraries*, xiv, xviii, 20, 21, 22, 51, 53, 54, 56, 73, 76, 79; *Information Literacy Competency Standards for Higher Education*, xvi, 10, 41, 44, 45; *Roles and Strengths of Teaching Librarians*, 1–2, 36, 37, 61, 68, 120; *Standards for Libraries in Higher Education*, 75–76, 84, 117; *Standards for Proficiencies for Instruction Librarians and Coordinators*, 15n1; *See also Framework for Information Literacy for Higher Education*
astray, going, xviii, 10, 87, 89, 90, 100, 103

benchmarking, xvii, 18, 22, 63, 71, 78, 79–80
burnout, xviii, 100–101, 110; identifying, 100, 108; in Instruction Coordinators, 11, 103, 105–107, 109, 116; recovering from, 108, 109; in teaching librarians, 90, 101

campus climate, 2, 22, 67, 80, 97, 117
card sorting, 96
co-curricular, 25, 47, 55, 68, 75; building relationships, 25, 85; engaging students, 47, 68, 75; outreach opportunities, 55,

68
collaboration, 2, 67, 70, 79, 91, 99, 102, 112; among instruction librarians, 35, 44, 83, 101, 106; supporting student learning, xviii, 6, 52, 65, 68, 85; on teaching, xviii, 6, 21, 25, 27, 31, 79, 113. *See also* partnerships
communities: learning, 115, 118, 123; of practice, xvi, xviii, 34–35, 38, 112
conflict: addressing, 12, 90; interpersonal, 12, 90, 100, 101–102; priorities, 20
coordinating, ix, xv, 2, 4, 31–32, 61, 106, 108, 112, 113, 115, 116. *See also* Instruction Coordinators
culture: campus, 24–25, 26, 71, 74, 83, 90, 99–100, 120; defining, 29, 33, 102; of growth, 14, 97; inclusive, x, 2, 19, 102, 121; interpersonal, 101–102, 103; of teaching and learning, xv–xvi, 4, 6, 15, 18, 20, 23, 27–28, 30–31, 32, 33, 34, 37, 39, 53, 54, 79, 84, 85, 89, 118, 119
curriculum map(ping), 26, 41, 43, 45, 46, 68, 70, 77, 78, 79, 81

development, 12, 86, 115–116; personal, Coordinators, xviii, 8, 11, 105, 107, 109, 110–111; pedagogical, 47, 48, 49, 50, 56, 75, 77, 85, 105; professional, instruction librarians, xiii, xv, xvi, 4, 14, 23, 32, 48, 79, 81, 85, 101, 112–114, 115; team, 14, 23, 30, 35, 37, 44, 47, 98. *See also* instruction programs, development of; leadership
diagnosing problems, xviii, 90, 91
difficult: conversations, 96–98; questions, 92–96
digital scholarship, xvi, 4, 32, 35
diversity, 120; commitment to, 57, 58; instruction program context, 1, 8, 37, 69, 117, 118; of learners, 53, 70. *See also* Association of College and Research Libraries, *Diversity Standards: Cultural Competency for Academic Libraries*; inclusive

embedded: information literacy, xviii, 1, 52, 74, 119, 120; leadership, 116; librarians, 24, 69, 79

emotional intelligence, characteristics of, 7–8, 10–11, 91, 100–101, 106. *See also* leadership
empathy, 7, 8, 9, 10–11, 14, 106, 109
evaluation. *See* assessment

failure, 103, 108, 113
flexibility, x, 10, 37, 43, 45, 48, 66, 103, 109
Four Frames (Bolman & Deal), 90–91, 92, 108; academic leadership and the, 90–92, 100; library instruction programs and the, 98–100
Framework for Information Literacy for Higher Education, xvi, xvii, 10, 20, 37, 41–42, 49, 50, 53, 57, 124; alternatives to, 45–48, 77; critiques of the, 10, 43, 44; instruction programs and the, 28, 42, 43, 53, 81; student learning assessment and the, 43; threshold concepts and the, 44–45, 49

growth: Instruction Coordinators', 11, 14–15, 92, 105, 107, 108, 109–110, 112, 113, 115, 116; instruction librarians', 6, 12, 34, 35, 38, 68, 75; of instruction programs, 65, 69, 72, 74, 79, 87, 92, 103, 120; students', 4, 117

holistic thinking, xiv, 9, 19, 21, 25, 28, 49, 74, 80, 115–116, 120

inclusive: culture, x, 55, 57, 58, 80, 83, 121; library staff, xiii, 56; program development, xvii, 55; teaching practices, 57, 58. *See also* diversity
information literacy. *See* accreditation; Association of College and Research Libraries; curriculum map(ping); embedded, information literacy; *Framework for Information Literacy for Higher Education*; lifelong learning; pedagogy
Instruction Coordinators: dispositions of, xvi, 2, 6, 8, 10, 11, 14, 15, 106; varieties of, xv, 4, 14, 62, 96, 121. *See also* advocacy, a Coordinator's role in; assessment of Instruction Coordinators; burnout in Instruction Coordinators;

coordinating; development, personal, Coordinators'; growth, Instruction Coordinators'; toughness, Instruction Coordinators'; vision of Instruction Coordinators

instruction. *See* culture, teaching and learning; pedagogy; instruction librarians; instruction programs

instruction librarians, x, xvii, 2, 6, 17, 29, 34, 41, 44, 46, 61, 62, 63, 79, 83, 89, 101, 105, 106, 107; development of, xvi, 4, 6, 21, 22, 24, 30, 34, 37, 38, 48, 81, 85, 101, 115, 124; evaluation of, 52, 54, 73, 80, 84, 110; identity of, xviii, 2, 14, 20, 30, 32, 34, 35, 89, 90, 96, 98, 101, 102; role in teaching and learning, xvii, 22–23, 26, 34, 49, 55, 56, 59, 61, 65, 67, 73, 74, 75, 86, 87, 98, 102, 117, 119, 120. *See also* Association of College and Research Libraries, *Roles and Strengths of Teaching Librarians*; Stakeholders

instruction programs: development of, 21, 22, 27, 28, 29, 31, 39, 42, 43, 44, 46, 50, 54, 55, 56, 70, 72, 78, 83, 85, 90; mission of, 26, 29, 43, 53, 56, 57, 61, 66, 84, 90, 99, 118; revision, 22, 53, 72, 73, 76, 77, 100; structure of, xvi, xviii, 1, 2, 19, 21, 27–28, 34, 42, 44, 45, 48, 49, 63. *See also* advocacy for instruction programs; assessment of instruction programs; marketing; mission, educational; value of instruction programs; vision, instruction program strategic planning

instructional design, 68, 80, 121

instructional leadership. *See* leadership, instructional

intentionality, xv, xviii, 14–15, 33, 43, 58, 59, 72, 85, 92, 97, 103, 105, 109, 110, 115–116

leadership: academic, 90, 91, 92, 108; development of, ix, 110–111; emotional intelligence, 7–8, 10–11, 91, 100–101, 106; instructional, 5–6; servant, 8, 106–107; teaching as, 4, 5–6

library instruction. *See* assessment of student learning; curriculum map(ping);

Instruction Coordinators; instruction librarians; instruction programs; value of instruction programs

lifelong learning, 38, 45, 49, 53, 69, 81, 117, 119

management, xv, 2, 4, 5, 7, 11, 17, 32, 57, 87, 91, 92, 101, 103, 110, 123. *See also* leadership

marketing, xiii, xvii, 21, 59, 62, 63, 64, 69, 73, 121. *See also* advocacy

mission: educational, xviii, 5, 9, 23, 32, 55, 56, 58, 102, 117; library, 52, 78, 100, 118, 119; statements, xiii, 20, 22, 51, 53, 56, 63, 83, 119, 121; university, 25, 52, 53, 54, 87. *See also* instruction programs, mission of; statement of purpose

needs assessment. *See* assessment, needs analysis

Open Educational Resources (OER), 38, 42

openness, 11, 13, 22, 48, 96, 121

partnerships, xvii, xviii, 87, 98, 99, 119; with administrators, 26, 66, 118; building, xviii, 23, 55, 64, 65, 85; on campus, 68, 99; with faculty, x, 1, 23, 24, 25, 48, 67, 70, 89; with librarians, x, 65; with students, 56, 69–70; teaching and learning, 5, 17, 31, 48, 61, 79, 117, 119, 120–121. *See also* collaboration

pedagogy, ix, xvi, 4–5, 24, 26, 31, 37, 81; critical, 57–58, 124

Personal Learning Networks (PLNs), 112–113, 115

Personal Strategic Plan(ning) (PSP), 111

reflective practice, xvi, 12, 14, 15, 34, 38, 43, 50, 53, 70, 96, 103, 110, 111, 114, 116

renewal, 109, 110

resources, xiii, 10, 22, 35, 71, 75, 77, 87, 109, 115, 121, 124; allocation of, 19, 21, 27, 75, 80, 85, 98, 99, 101, 118; instruction program, xvi, 22–23, 41, 51, 74, 100; managing, 2, 3, 31, 32, 66, 84,

90, 118. *See also* Open Educational Resources (OER)

Sacrifice Syndrome, 108, 110
Scholarship of Teaching and Learning (SoTL), x, 33–34, 48, 85, 114, 121, 123, 124
signature pedagogies, 47–48, 77
social justice framework, 57–58
spaces, instructional, 3, 22, 74–75, 79, 80, 85
stakeholders, 15, 18, 27, 31, 62, 63, 65, 70, 91, 117; on campus, 2, 6, 23, 24, 53, 56, 58, 86, 120; communicating value, 70, 71, 100, 118; expectations, 72, 98; feedback, 77, 84, 86, 110; learners, 14, 50, 51, 53, 57, 65, 69, 117, 120; in the library, 19, 30, 63, 65, 119. *See also* administration; administrators; instruction librarians
statement of purpose, 20, 21, 51, 53; revision, 53, 72. *See also* mission, statements; vision, statements
strategic: alignment, 4, 83, 98, 103; initiatives, 25, 36, 55, 73, 74, 91; plan(ning), 2, 12, 18, 19, 27, 28, 57, 66, 79, 96, 120; risk taking, 10, 98. *See also* Personal Strategic Plan(ning) (PSP)
student learning. *See* assessment; lifelong learning; stakeholders, learners
SWOT Analysis, 96

teaching. *See* culture, teaching and learning; pedagogy; instruction librarians; instruction programs
teaching and learning programs. *See* instruction programs
teaching librarians. *See* instruction librarians
threshold concepts, 44–45. *See also Framework for Information Literacy for Higher Education*
toughness, in Instruction Coordinators', 11–12

Universal Design for Learning, 57, 84

value: communicating, 27, 48, 61–62, 68, 70, 71, 73, 87; demonstrating, 3, 52, 66–67, 70, 83, 86; of instruction programs, 20, 26, 51, 69, 74; shared amongst librarians, 4, 8, 20, 29, 32, 38, 39, 47, 48, 99, 110, 111, 115, 119
vision, 5, 6, 7, 18, 25, 33, 55, 59, 76; articulating for teaching and learning, xiv, xvii, 3, 50, 52, 54, 121; for the future, 119–120; of Instruction Coordinators, 109, 111; instruction program strategic planning, 29, 43, 55, 65, 120; misalignment, 99–100; statements, xiii, 20, 51, 52, 63, 121. *See also* statement of purpose

About the Author

Melissa N. Mallon is the director of the Peabody Education Library at Vanderbilt University, and director of Teaching and Learning for the Vanderbilt Libraries, which includes planning and directing systemwide involvement in campus teaching and learning initiatives including strategies for the development of information literacy instruction, library involvement in assessment of student learning, and training and mentoring of library staff.

Mallon received her master's in library and information science from Louisiana State University. Before joining Vanderbilt in 2015, Mallon was a faculty member and instruction coordinator at the University of Pittsburgh-Johnstown and Wichita State University. She has published, presented, and taught professional development courses in the areas of digital and information literacies, online learning, the Scholarship of Teaching & Learning, and creative use of emerging technologies in assessing student learning. Her previous books include *The Pivotal Role of Academic Librarians in Digital Learning* (Libraries Unlimited, 2017), and she co-edited the book, *The Grounded Instruction Librarian: Participating in the Scholarship of Teaching and Learning* (ACRL, 2019).